Documents a
The Origins of the S

Documents and Debates
General Editor: John Wroughton M.A., F.R.Hist.S.

The Origins of the Second World War

Victor Mallia-Milanes M.A., Ph.D., F.R.Hist.S.

Acting-Head, History, The New Lyceum (Arts), Malta

MACMILLAN

First published 1987
Reprinted 1989

Published by
MACMILLAN EDUCATION LTD
Houndmills, Basingstoke, Hampshire RG21 2XS
and London
Companies and representatives
throughout the world

Typeset by Wessex Typesetters
(Division of The Eastern Press Ltd)
Frome, Somerset

Printed in Hong Kong

ISBN 0–333–40881–0

The cover illustration shows Adolf Hitler in Munich in 1928.
Reproduced by kind permission of Bildarchiv Preussischer
Kulturbesitz.

Contents

General Editor's Preface

This book forms part of a series entitled *Documents and Debates*, which is aimed primarily at sixth formers. The earlier volumes in the series each covered approximately one century of history, using material both from original documents and from modern historians. The more recent volumes, however, are designed in response to the changing trends in history examinations at 18 plus, most of which now demand the study of documentary sources and the testing of historical skills. Each volume therefore concentrates on a particular topic within a narrower span of time. It consists of eight sections, each dealing with a major theme in depth, illustrated by extracts drawn from primary sources. The series intends partly to provide experience for those pupils who are required to answer questions on documentary material at A-level, and partly to provide pupils of all abilities with a digestible and interesting collection of source material, which will extend the normal textbook approach.

This book is designed essentially for the pupil's own personal use. The author's introduction will put the period as a whole into perspective, highlighting the central issues, main controversies, available source material and recent developments. Although it is clearly not our intention to replace the traditional textbook, each section will carry its own brief introduction, which will set the documents into context. A wide variety of source material has been used in order to give the pupils the maximum amount of experience – letters, speeches, newspapers, memoirs, diaries, official papers, Acts of Parliament, Minute Books, accounts, local documents, family papers, etc. The questions vary in difficulty, but aim throughout to compel the pupil to think in depth by the use of unfamiliar material. Historical knowledge and understanding will be tested, as well as basic comprehension. Pupils will also be encouraged by the questions to assess the reliability of evidence, to recognise bias and emotional prejudice, to reconcile conflicting accounts and to extract the essential from the irrelevant. Some questions, *marked with an asterisk*, require knowledge outside the immediate extract and are intended for further research or discussion, based on the pupil's general knowledge of the period. Finally, we hope that students using this material will learn something of the nature of historical inquiry and the role of the historian.

John Wroughton

Acknowledgements

The author and publishers wish to thank the following who have kindly given permission for the use of copyright material:

Allen & Unwin for extracts from *The Struggle for the Danube and the Little Entente* by Robert Machray and from *The Fascist Challenge and the Policy of Appeasement* by J. Wolfgang et al.; Edward Arnold for extracts from *Hitler: A Study in Personality and Politics* and *A History of Germany 1815–1945*, both books by William Carr; Ernest Benn for an extract from *The Road to Prosperity* by Sir George Paish; Bodley Head for an extract from *Will War Come in Europe?* by H. R. Knickerbocker; BPC Publishing Ltd for an extract from *History of the 20th Century*; Brace and Company for an extract from *Peacemaking 1919* by Harold Nicolson; Frank Cass & Co. Ltd for extracts from *France and the Coming of the Second World War 1936–39* by Anthony Adamthwaite; Cassell Ltd for extracts from volume I of *The Second World War* by Winston S. Churchill; Century Hutchinson Publishing Group for extracts from *Mein Kampf* by Adolf Hitler (Hurst & Blackett, 1939), trans. J. Murphy; Chapman & Hall Ltd for extracts from *Five Years of European Chaos* by Maxwell H. H. Macartney; Collins Publishers for an extract from *Duce! The Rise and Fall of Benito Mussolini* by Richard Collier; Constable Publishers for extracts from *An English Wife in Berlin* by Evelyn Princess Blücher, *After the War: A Diary* by Lieut.-Col C. à Court Repington and *The Peace Negotiations: A Personal Narrative* by Robert Lansing; Doubleday & Co. Inc. for an extract from *Woodrow Wilson and World Settlement* by R. Stannard Baker; Eyre Methuen Ltd for extracts from *Hitler Speaks: A Series of Political Conversations with Adolf Hitler on his Real Aims* by Hermann Rauschning; Eyre & Spottiswoode (Publishers) Ltd for an extract from *Franco: A Biographical History* by Brian Crozier; Fawcett World Library for extracts from the second edition of *The Origins of the Second World War* by A. J. P. Taylor; Robert Hale Ltd for an extract from *A New Holy Alliance* by Emil Ludwig; Hamish Hamilton Ltd for extracts from *The Time for Decision* by Sumner Welles; Harper and Brothers for an extract from *The House that Hitler Built* by S. H. Roberts; D. C. Heath & Company for an extract from *The Ethiopian Crisis: Touchstone of Appeasement?* ed. Ludwig F. Schaefer; William Heinemann Ltd for an extract from *The*

Memoirs of General the Lord Ismay; Her Majesty's Stationery Office for extracts from *British and Foreign State Papers*, volume CXL (1936) and from volume III of *Documents of European Economic History* eds Sidney Pollard and Colin Holmes; Insel Verlag for extracts from *The Diaries of a Cosmopolitan: Count Harry Kessler 1918–1937* trans. and ed. Charles Kessler; Longman Group UK Limited for an extract from *History of England* by G. M. Trevelyan; Professor Daniel D. McGarry for an extract from *Sources of Western Civilization* by D. D. McGarry *et al.*; Methuen & Co. Ltd for an extract from *The Hitler I Knew* by Otto Dietrich; Macmillan Publishing Company (New York) for extracts from *Munich: Before and After* by W. W. Hadley; Martin Secker & Warburg Ltd for extracts from *The Rise and Fall of the Third Reich* by William Shirer; Oxford University Press for extracts from *Documents in the Political History of the European Continent 1815–1919*, ed. G. A. Kertesz, *World History from 1914 to 1961* by David Thomson; *God's Playground: A History of Poland* by Norman Davies, and *Making the Fascist State* by H. W. Schneider; Penguin Books Ltd for extracts from *Hitler: A Study in Tyranny* by Alan Bullock, *Europe and the Czechs* by S. Grant Duff, *Europe since Napoleon* by David Thomson, *My Life: An Attempt at an Autobiography* by Leon Trotsky, *The Long Weekend* by Robert Graves and Alan Hodge, *Diaries and Letters 1930–1964* by Harold Nicolson, edited and condensed by Stanley Olson, *Selected Prose* by T. S. Eliot, ed. John Hayward, and *From Versailles to Wall Street* by Derek H. Aldcroft; Prentice-Hall, Inc. for an extract from *A Diplomatic History of the American People* by Thomas A. Bailey; The Custodian of the Public Record Office, London, for extracts from Foreign Office documents; Reynal & Hitchcock for an extract from *Adolf Hitler: My New Order* by R. de Roussy de Sales; Routledge & Kegan Paul Ltd for extracts from *The Foreign Policy of France from 1914 to 1945* by J. Néré, *The Great War 1914–1918* by Marc Ferro, *Italian Foreign Policy 1870–1940* by C. J. Lowe and F. Marzari, and *Fascist Italy* by Alan Cassels; The Royal Institute of International Affairs for an extract from *A Short History of International Affairs 1920–1939* by G. M. Gathorne-Hardy; The University of California for an extract from *Young Mussolini and the Intellectual Origins of Fascism* by A. James Gregor; Weidenfeld (Publishers) Ltd for extracts from *Mussolini* by Denis Mack Smith.

Every effort has been made to trace all the copyright holders but if any have been inadvertently overlooked the publishers will be pleased to make the necessary arrangement at the first opportunity.

The author is grateful to the librarians and staff of both the National Library and the University Library, Malta and to his friend Maurice Demarco.

The Origins of the Second World War

The peace settlements signed at Versailles after the First World War in June 1919 resulted in no real or lasting peace. At best they permitted an uneasy and precarious armistice which lasted scarcely twenty years. Europe was then plunged once more into that new and greater conflict known as the Second World War.

Sumner Welles, *Where are we heading?*

It is one of history's major ironies that the origins of the Second World War are generally traced to the way the statesmen at the Paris Conference in 1919 tried to elicit permanent peace and order out of the chaos in which both victors and defeated languished. The task of reconstruction had been formidable. Amid widely divergent cultural attitudes, the early postwar years were replete with high-sounding professions of faith and noble principles, with discordant follies, blunders and contradictions, with disconcerting problems and disappointed aspirations, with vindictive decisions that were almost 'foredoomed to failure'.

The unwise partition of the Habsburg monarchy, 'a stabilising influence in south-eastern Europe', into little, independent and defenceless 'succession states' revived the old medieval *Drang nach Osten* objective of the Germans. With Russia diminished and withdrawn into revolutionary isolation, the peacemakers unwittingly rendered more feasible the realisation of the innate German desire to expand eastward. By reducing 'the former Habsburg metropolis to the proportions of a dwarf, the Allies were virtually offering Austria to Germany as a gift' (Marc Ferro). Sumner Welles called the Polish Corridor 'a fatal mistake'. Were not the decisions to separate the 'indisputably German city' of Danzig from Germany and to 'attribute' the Sudeten German population to Czechoslovakia and the 'Magyars of Transylvania' to Roumania equally so? It appears that the Allies' belief in the principle of national self-determination was less influential in determining the final peace settlement than their desire to create a new balance of power. They grossly underestimated Japanese and Italian discontent. They mistook the 'national rage' of the Germans for a temporary 'sign of defeat'. Versailles had remorselessly forced upon Berlin the bitter experience of what has been termed 'the full reality of defeat': the loss of continental and overseas territories, army reduction, the confiscation of their fleet and severe reparations. The occupation of the left bank of the Rhine for fifteen years was intended to allay the French obsession with security and guarantee fulfilment of Treaty obligations. But unlike the Habsburg monarchy, Germany was spared drastic partition and was cynically allowed to enjoy the potential of 'the most powerful European continental state' (Grenville). Were the peacemakers in fact 'losing the peace at the moment they won the war'? It was in Germany that the grievances generated by the settlement found their major driving force. From 'the moment [Adolf Hitler] became a political agitator', they found in him a hysterical revanchist voice of restless protest and ruthless revisionism.

Under the pervasive influence of Woodrow Wilson's political philosophy, it was believed at the time that peace could be preserved and reconciliation of all present and future conflicting interests achieved through the international machinery of the League of Nations. What was not appreciated then was that if 'the combination of power needed to achieve Germany's collapse in 1918, without which a Treaty on the lines of Versailles could never have been imposed, did not remain available to uphold its terms' (Michael Balfour), the prospects of consolidating the peace would be poor indeed. In this sense one of the heaviest blows to the League came from the United States. The American Senate first declined to ratify it and then, eventually, retreated to isolationism.

With the exception of a few isolated outbursts of dissension, the undercurrents of resentment and discontent remained subdued during the next decade. The twenties were years of relative calm, marked by what appeared to be a sense of political stability, economic recovery and promising self-confidence. Peaceful diplomacy succeeded in fostering international cooperation among the more important nations of the world, leading from the Dawes Plan to the Locarno Agreements, Germany's entry into the League of Nations, the Pact of Paris and the Young Plan. But the inner ferment and unease of European society were forcibly manifesting themselves in novel artistic attitudes and literary styles whose discordance with established norms and values called all accepted realities in doubt. The 'disaffected intelligentsia' sought to explore unconventional modes of expression, free of all traditional restraints and, in so doing, glorified the unorthodox, the irrational, the subconscious. Was this intellectual and artistic aspiration to distort known reality and reveal the moral bankruptcy of society a sour foretaste of the violent upheaval ahead?

In October 1929 the onset of the Great Depression shattered economic recovery. There was a catastrophic decline in world trade, international investment 'virtually ceased' and it became 'increasingly difficult' to balance international accounts 'long before the financial panic swept so many currencies off the gold standard' (*World Economic Survey 1932–33*). There was heavy widespread unemployment everywhere. The promising Locarno era was suddenly replaced by economic warfare, which led rapidly to a chain of developments that 'reinforced the division of the world' and underscored the inherent powerlessness of the League of Nations as an international peacekeeping body. The great depression, and the consequences of the depression, caused 'a sinister transformation' of the entire international atmosphere. Growth of autarky, massive rearmament, unrestrained aggression, failure of 'collective security' and a provocative disregard of the League became the characteristic features of the 1930s. Japan defied the League in 1931 and left it two years later over the issue of Manchuria. Mussolini outdared the League in 1935 when he invaded Abyssinia, thereby creating a chasm between Fascist Italy and the western democracies. Adolf Hitler 'defied the entire system of international relations when he repudiated the Versailles system in 1935' and, in defiance of all treaty obligations, occupied the Rhineland in 1936, denouncing the Locarno Treaty which he had voluntarily signed. 'No one lifted a finger to stop' Nazi Germany (Lord Ismay) or any other aggressor. Or if they did, they did so halfheartedly. The division of the world became further pronounced during the civil war in Spain, with the Fascist regimes supporting the rebels, the Soviet Union backing the legitimate Republican government, and the western Allies defending passively the principle of nonintervention. This politico-ideological division was consolidated by the formation first of the Rome–Berlin Axis and then by the Fascist Rome–Berlin–Tokyo Triangle when Mussolini joined the Anti-Comintern Pact in November 1937. The western democracies never enjoyed the benefits of a formal alliance with the United States.

The student of the later interwar period would do well to reflect on whether it was Nazi Germany's aggression and her barefaced defiance of all international accords or the highly controversial policy of appeasement pursued by Britain and France that ultimately led to the achievement of Hitler's 'brilliant and bloodless successes' from his first coup in March 1936 to his fifth on 22 March 1939. In his *Memoirs* Lord Ismay recorded his impressions of the western powers' reaction to Hitler's *Anschluss* with Austria:

It was a sign of the times that this example of rapine was almost taken for granted. Russia's proposal to have a conference was ignored. France contented herself with reaffirming her guarantee to Czechoslovakia. Great Britain, who had always contemplated some sort of union between Germany and Austria, did nothing except register disapproval of Hitler's methods. And Mussolini, so far from moving troops to the Brenner Pass, earned Hitler's undying gratitude by his acquiescence in the Anschluss.

It was a perfect replica of the western attitude to the Nazi remilitarisation of the Rhineland and would be repeated at least once more at Munich in 1938. The advocates of the European status quo seemed to have lost all sense of urgency. In the context of Hitler's fearless drive against all odds, appeasement has often been considered a symptom of decadence, a policy of weakness and surrender which convinced the *Führer* 'that neither [Britain] nor France' was 'capable of fighting a war'. Was appeasement in fact motivated by an inherent hatred of war or by a realistic awareness of military unpreparedness? Or was it the fear of the revolutionary contagion of Bolshevism, traced back perhaps to Béla Kun's success, that induced, if not compelled, Britian and France to appease the dictators? If so, it was a grievous fault. Welles called the belief 'that democracy and Communism cannot simultaneously exist in the world' an 'insane delusion'.

'[T]he causes' of the Second World War, says Taylor, 'are embarrassingly many'. It is not the purpose of this book to assign responsibility or blame for the occurrence of the war to any particular event or sequence of events. It is intended rather to study the 'antecedents' that are generally recognised as relevant to its outbreak in Europe on 1 September 1939 without attributing to them any causal status, to diagnose through the close study of documentary evidence the conditions, attitudes, ideas and personalities which, both in their individual capacity and through their collective interrelationship, moulded the interwar period. Each of the eight sections below concentrates on a major theme. This, it is hoped, will allow the student to form his own causal judgements, establish his own 'hierarchy of causes' and arrive leisurely at *his* interpretation.

Abundant official diplomatic documentation is now available in various languages. Other primary source material is easily accessible in the form of memoirs of leading personalities, very often published 'to justify themselves', diaries, speeches of statesmen and politicians, autobiographies, contemporary or near-contemporary accounts of events and collections of private correspondence. An intelligent use of the press as a gauge of public opinion is certain to yield excellent results.

There is also an extensively rich secondary literature in English, including articles in learned journals, on nearly all major aspects of the interwar years. Of outstanding significance is A. J. P. Taylor's *The Origins of the Second World War*, if only for the debate which it had so fiercely provoked and the profound impact it has made on historical thinking. A quarter-century after its first publication in

1961, it still guarantees 'exciting and fascinating' reading. Equally stimulating and generously rewarding to the student of the international relations between the two world wars are the views of Taylor's major critics exposed in the collections of essays on the Second World War edited by Esmonde M. Robertson (1971), W. Roger Lewis (1972) and Gordon Martel (1986).

I Hopes, Fears and Follies 1919–23

Introduction

Two distinct forms of idealism – Wilsonism and Bolshevism – enlightened the final peace settlement in 1919, the one through seeming admiration, the other through genuine fear.

The principles of universal democracy and national self-determination, enshrined in Wilson's celebrated 'Fourteen Points' constituted the first Utopian vision. Abhorring the futility and inhumanity of the recent experience, this vision was to form the bedrock of the final settlement and the Covenant of the League of Nations, whose raison d'être was 'to restrict war and make peace more positive'. Wilsonism was however as unrealistic as it was controversial. How would such broad principles placate the tigerish fury of Clemenceau? How far can it be deemed democratic to impose a democratic form of government upon a nation where responsible parliamentary government had no tradition? What real chances of survival, if not efficiency, could it have?

Bolshevism, on the other hand, loomed 'larger in men's minds and fears in 1919 than anything else in the post-war world' (Thomson). Internal revolutions and military catastrophe had not only driven Russia out of the war; they turned her out of Europe. But though in the western view Russia ceased to exist as a great power, her new political ideology still haunted Europe 'as a spectre' (Taylor). Were not the Spartacists in Germany and Béla Kun's regime in Hungary clear enough evidence? The dissolution of the Habsburg Empire into its component racial fragments further confined Russia by means of a *cordon sanitaire* into a state of isolationism. But was not this a case of mutual exclusion?

The final peace settlement 'failed to ensure a peaceful future'. It had included 'no provisions for the economic rehabilitation of Europe, nothing to make the defeated Central Empires into good neighbours, nothing to stabilize the new States of Europe, nothing to reclaim Russia' (Keynes). The years 1919–23 betray its unworkability and short-sightedness. Germany had been decisively reduced to an impotent nation, 'defeated, disarmed and hungry' (Churchill) and, by the forced acceptance of the *diktat*, most profoundly humiliated. But she was neither destroyed nor disunited. Her threatening potential, even if largely psychological at this stage, forced France, obsessed with security and reparations, to seek guarantees against aggression in a series of mutual alliances with the 'successor states' and, eventually, to occupy the Ruhr. Italy's uproar over her claim to Fiume not only underscored the inherent flaws of secret diplomacy; it soon led to D'Annuncio's escapade and Mussolini's 'March on Rome'.

In any attempt to assess the soundness of the 1919 settlement other important questions arise. Why was Paris, the capital of a country 'bled white by the war', chosen as the venue for the Peace Conference, and not, for example, neutral Geneva? Was the application of the principle of self-determination the realisation of an ideal which the peacemakers ardently believed in, or simply a *fait accompli* which they could not but accept and recognise? To what extent was the attitude adopted towards Germany at Versailles genuinely objective, just and realistic? To what extent was it innately vindictive to satisfy the prevailing temper and bitter resentment of the suffering masses? It was the masses after all who had given Clemenceau, Lloyd George and Orlando 'an emphatic mandate . . . that the enemy must be made to pay' – a psychological reward for their sufferings. In the final resort, could the Allies in fact reject Wilson's guiding vision, or was it, too, imposed upon them when their economic dependence on the United States at this point in time left them hardly any room for choice?

It has also been argued in favour of the peacemakers that 'many of the ills of Europe' followed 'straight from the war, not from the peace', and therefore the enormous changes which the war had introduced – territorial, economic and social – could neither be controlled nor, still less, could they be arrested.

1 The Spectre of Bolshevism

Bolshevism has become a force to be reckoned with. It threatens us through the Red Army, which is to be brought up to a million men in strength, and there are dreams of setting up soviet régimes first throughout the old Russian territories and then in the rest of
5 Europe. This new and monstrous form of imperialism will threaten Europe all the more fearsome as it comes precisely at the end of the war, which will inevitably provoke, in all countries, a serious economic and social crisis . . . . The Allies must therefore cause the soviets to collapse. This will not be achieved by carrying
10 the war to Russia, but rather through economic encirclement of Bolshevism . . . occupation by Allied troops from Romania, Odessa and the rest, of the Crimea and Ukrainian corn belts and the Donets coal-basin, which will be vital pledges for the payment

of the 26,000,000,000 we have lent Russia, and which the
15 Bolsheviks have repudiated . . . the armies of the Balkans, British
armies in Turkey will, after the Turks have given in, furnish the
few divisions needed to establish, around Bolshevism, not only a
cordon sanitaire to isolate it and kill it by starvation, but also the
nuclei of friendly forces around which the healthy elements of
20 Russia will be able to organize, and bring about the renovation of
their country under the aegis of the Entente.

> Georges Clemenceau's plan to contain Bolshevism,
> described to Pichon on 23 October 1918. Document
> reproduced in Marc Ferro, *The Great War 1914–1918*, trans.
> Nicole Stone (London, Routledge & Kegan Paul, 1973),
> pp. 212–13

Questions

★ *a* How real, in your opinion, was the threat of Bolshevism to
Europe in 1918?

 b 'From October [1918] a clear distinction was being drawn
between the struggle against the Central Powers and the
struggle against Bolshevism, which hitherto had been lumped
together' (Ferro). Discuss this view in the light of the above
extract.

★ *c* How wise, do you think, was Clemenceau's appeal for a
'crusade' against Bolshevism? What chances did 'the healthy
elements of Russia' (lines 19–20) have in October 1918 of
bringing 'about the renovation of their country' (lines 20–21)?

★ *d* To what extent, and in what ways, were Clemenceau's fears
justified in the early postwar years?

2 Germany in 1918: an English view

Krieblowitz, December 1918. . . . I am beginning to comprehend
that the war with its orgy of death and slaughter has come to an
end. It is especially hard to realize, because the difficulties of
every-day life are almost greater now than they were before – or
5 seem so. The whole economic organization of Germany has
crumbled away before our eyes, and no new system has as yet
been formed in its place. The revolution, in fact, came too
suddenly, even for the Socialists themselves, and what ought to
have evolved from a natural course of events was prematurely
10 hurled at us by the unexpected insurrection of the sailors in Kiel
and Hamburg. Therefore the Socialists have not had time to
develop a really strong Government, or to test the practical
working of theories in a country which is still at heart for the
greater part monarchical in its sympathies.
15   I believe myself that the German people in reality need

something for their imagination – a figure-head that represents in some way the phantastic, the unusual, the ideal. There is no poetry in the figure of a short stout President, with a bald head, a top-hat, and a black coat. . . .

20   Germany's chief danger at the moment is her lack of a central strong Government to negotiate with the Entente, and to take the lead in the land. Instead of one there is a whole series of governments, and no end to the bickerings and jealousies between the different states, which are all aiming at reducing the power of
25   Berlin. At the moment the proletariat are in possession of power, which they are using to enrich themselves as speedily as possible at the cost of the nation. I hear, if things go on as they are, the State will be bankrupt in a fortnight. . . .

The nation at large is economically demoralised and corrupted
30   by the organizations of militarism. . . .

Another problem is what is to become of all the active officers who are being dismissed, and who in civil life have learnt nothing at all? Germany, with no power to expand, and morally blockaded by the rest of the world for years to come, offers but a disconsolate
35   future for young men, however enterprising they may be. The French ideal, 'l'esclavage allemand', seems the only possible solution, if the Entente insist on the conditions they are proposing.

Little miseries which seemed but pin-pricks a short time ago are gradually gaining in intensity, until they feel almost like poisonous
40   darts. For years people have been struggling along, supporting as best they could the absence of everything conducive to a decent existence, but now it is almost impossible to bear it any longer. The ancient boots and shoes defy any more mending, the stockings consist of a series of variegated patches, dresses and mantles have
45   been turned and dyed year after year, and most people's underwear has no recognizable resemblance to the dainty garments of pre-war times. They are of a nameless hue, and look as if they had been fished out of some forgotten patch-bag. As there is no soap, our linen issues from the wash-tub greyer and more hopelessly
50   torn than we ever dared imagine, and certainly the German woman of to-day is the worst clad in all Europe.

It is a sorry outlook for Christmas, and not even the children will be able to indulge in any of the little luxuries which the 'Weihnachtsmann' usually left at their door.

Evelyn, Princess Blücher, *An English Wife in Berlin: A private memoir of events, politics and daily life in Germany throughout the war and the social revolution of 1918* (London, Constable & Co. Ltd, 1920), pp 302–4

Questions

a   Explain and comment on (i) 'The whole economic organization . . . in its place.' (lines 5–7); (ii) 'the unexpected insurrection of the sailors in Kiel and Hamburg' (lines 10–11); (iii) 'to test the practical working of theories' (lines 12–13); (iv) 'the organizations of militarism' (line 30).

  b Do you agree with Blücher that Germany in 1918 was largely 'monarchical in its sympathies' (line 14)? If so, why was the Hohenzollern regime replaced by the Weimar Republic? What chances did Germany have in 1918–19 of going Bolshevist?

  c Suggest what Blücher had in mind when she wrote 'The French ideal . . . proposing.' (lines 35–7).

  d What contribution does the extract from Blücher's *memoir* make to your impression of Germany towards the end of 1918? What other sources would you consult to check the reliability, or otherwise, of her observations?

3   Two forms of idealism

(a) Wilson's apocalypse – The Fourteen Points

1. Open covenants of peace openly arrived at . . .

2. Absolute freedom of navigation . . . alike in peace and in war . . .

3. The removal . . . of all economic barriers and the establishment
5 of an equality of trade conditions among all the nations consenting to the peace . . .

4. . . . national armaments will be reduced to the lowest point consistent with domestic safety.

5. . . . impartial adjustment of all colonial claims based upon . . .
10 the principle that . . . the interests of the populations concerned must have equal weight with the . . . claims of the Government whose title is to be determined.

6. The evacuation of all Russian territory . . . as will secure the . . . co-operation of the other nations . . . for . . . an unhampered
15 and unembarrassed opportunity for the independent determination of her own political development and national policy, and assure her of a sincere welcome into the society of free nations under institutions of her own choosing . . .

7. Belgium . . . must be evacuated and restored without any
20 attempt to limit the sovereignty which she enjoys in common with all other free nations . . .

8. All French territory should be freed, and the invaded portions restored, and the wrong done to France by Prussia in 1871 in the matter of Alsace-Lorraine . . . should be righted . . .
25 9. A readjustment of the frontiers of Italy . . .

10. The peoples of Austria–Hungary . . . should be accorded . . . autonomous development.

11. Rumania, Serbia, and Montenegro should be evacuated;

occupied territories restored; Serbia accorded free access to the sea;
30   and the relations of the several Balkan States to one another
determined . . . along historically established lines of allegiance
and nationality . . . .
12. The Turkish portions of the present Ottoman Empire should
be assured a secure sovereignty, but the other nationalities which
35   are now under Turkish rule should be assured of . . . security of
life and . . . autonomous development, and the Dardanelles should
be permanently opened as a free passage to the ships and commerce
of all nations under international guarantees.
13. An independent Polish State should be erected which should
40   include the territories . . . indisputably Polish . . . .
14. A general association of nations must be formed . . . [to
afford] mutual guarantees of political independence and territorial
integrity to great and small states alike.
R. Stannard Baker, *Woodrow Wilson and World Settlement*,
vol III (New York, Doubleday, Page & Co., 1922) pp 42–5

(b) Pure democracy is sheer fraud. Lenin in 1919

The growth of the revolutionary movement of the proletariat in
45   all countries has called forth convulsive efforts of the bourgeoisie
and its agents in workmen's organisations, to find ideal political
arguments in defence of the rule of the exploiters. Among these
arguments stands out particularly condemnation of dictatorship
and defence of democracy. The falseness and hypocrisy of such an
50   argument, which has been repeated . . . at the conference of the
yellow International in February, 1919, Berne, are evident to all
who have not wished to betray the fundamental principle of
socialism.
First of all, this argument is used with certain interpretations of
55   'democracy in general' and 'dictatorship in general' without raising
the point as to which class one has in mind. Such a statement of
the question leaving out of consideration the question of class as
though it were a general national matter, is direct mockery of the
fundamental doctrine of socialism, namely, the doctrine of class
60   struggle, which the socialists who have gone over to the side of
the bourgeoisie recognize when they talk, but forget when they
act. For in no civilised capitalist country does there exist
'democracy in general,' but there exists only bourgeois democracy,
and one is speaking not of 'dictatorship in general' but of
65   dictatorship of the oppressed classes, that is, of the proletariat with
respect to the oppressors and exploiters, that is, the bourgeoisie,
in order to overcome the resistance which the exploiters make in
their struggle to preserve their rule.
History teaches that no oppressed class has ever come into
70   power and cannot come into power, without passing through a

period of dictatorship, that is, the conquest of power and the forcible suppression of the most desperate and mad resistance which does not hesitate to resort to any crimes, such has always been shown by the exploiters. The bourgeoisie, whose rule is now
75 defended by the socialists who speak against 'dictatorship in general', and who espouse the cause of 'democracy in general', has won power in the progressive countries at the price of a series of uprisings, civil wars . . . . The socialists of all countries . . . have explained to the people . . . the class character of these bourgeois
80 revolutions, and of this bourgeois dictatorship. Therefore the present defence of bourgeois democracy in the form of speeches about 'democracy in general', and the present wails and shouts against the dictatorship of the proletariat in the form of wails about 'dictatorship in general', are a direct mockery of socialism,
85 and represent in fact going over to the bourgeoisie and denying the right of the proletariat to its own proletariat revolution, and a defence of bourgeois reformism, precisely at the historic moment when bourgeois reformism is collapsing the world over, and when the war has created a revolutionary situation. . . .
90 Actual freedom and equality will exist only in the order established by the Communists, in which it will be impossible to become rich at the expense of another, where it will be impossible either directly or indirectly to subject the press to the power of money, where there will be an obstacle to prevent any toiler from
95 enjoying and actually realizing the equal right to the use of public printing presses and of the public fund of paper.

> Reproduced in *The World's Great Speeches*, ed. Lewis
> Copeland (New York, Garden City Publishers Co., 1942),
> pp 141–3

Questions

a Behind the 'Fourteen Points' lay 'Wilson's view of why the war [of 1914–18] had started.' He believed that 'by eliminating these causes war could be avoided'. Discuss these statements with particular reference to 'Points' 1–5 and 14 in the first extract.

b To what extent, and for what reasons, did the proposed territorial changes endorsed in 'Points' 6–13 (extract *a*) satisfy the Entente Allies?

★ c How far did the final peace settlement of 1919–20 reflect Wilson's vision? What other influences can you discern?

d Explain the historical context of Lenin's reference to (i) 'the yellow International' (lines 50–1); (ii) 'the socialists who have gone over to the side of the bourgeoisie' (lines 60–1); (iii) 'the historic moment . . . situation' (lines 87–9); (iv) the press (lines 90–6).

e In 1919 'all the Bolsheviks were far from being in agreement with the line proposed by Lenin' (Carrère D'Encausse). In the light of this statement, how far does extract *b* expose Lenin's fears and preoccupations in 1919?

f 'Wilson was as much a Utopian as Lenin' (Taylor). How far does this statement conform to the impression you have formed from the above two extracts?

4 The Paris Peace Conference: a postmortem

(a) The historian, with every justification, will come to the conclusion that we were very stupid men. I think we were. . . . We came to Paris confident that the new order was about to be established; we left it convinced that the new order had merely
5 fouled the old. . . . [T]his unhappy diminution of standard was very largely the fault . . . of democratic diplomacy.

We arrived determined that a Peace of justice and wisdom should be negotiated: we left it, conscious that the treaties imposed upon our enemies were neither just nor wise. . . . It is impossible
10 to read the German criticism without deriving the impression that the Paris Peace Conference was guilty of disguising an Imperialistic peace under the surface of Wilsonism, that seldom in the history of man has such vindictiveness cloaked itself in such unctuous sophistry. Hypocrisy was the predominant and unescapable result.
15 Yet was this hypocrisy wholly conscious, wholly deliberate? I do not think so. I certainly agree that the sanctimonious pharisaism of the Treaties is their gravest fault. . . . In the dust of controversy, in the rattle of time-pressure we lost all contact with our guiding stars. . . . We still desired ardently to maintain our principles
20 intact: it was only in the after-vacancy that we realised that they remained for us only in the form of empty words: it was then, and then only, that we faced the fact that the falsity of our position had led us into being false. It was by then too late. . . .

We had accepted a system for others which, when it came to
25 practice, we should refuse to apply to ourselves.
Harold Nicolson, *Peacemaking 1919* (New York, Harcourt, Brace & Co., 1939)

(b) The impression made by [the Treaty of Versailles] is one of disappointment, of regret, and of depression. The terms of peace appear immeasurably harsh and humiliating, while many of them seem to me impossible of performance.
30 The League of Nations created by the Treaty is relied upon to preserve the artificial structure which has been erected by compromise of the conflicting interests of the Great Powers and to prevent the germination of the seeds of war which are sown in so

many articles and which under normal conditions would soon
35 bear fruit. . . . Wars will come sooner or later.

It must be admitted in honesty that the League is an instrument
of the mighty to check the normal growth of national power and
national aspirations among those who have been rendered impotent
by defeat. Examine the Treaty and you will find peoples delivered
40 against their wills into the hands of those whom they hate, while
their economic resources are torn from them and given to others.
Resentment and bitterness, if not desperation, are bound to be the
consequences of such provisions. It may be years before these
oppressed peoples are able to throw off the yoke, but as sure as
45 day follows night the time will come when they will make the
effort.

This war was fought by the United States to destroy forever the
conditions which produced it. Those conditions have not been
destroyed. They have been supplanted by other conditions equally
50 productive of hatred, jealousy, and suspicion. In place of the
Triple Alliance and the Entente has risen the Quintuple Alliance
which is to rule the world. The victors in this war intend to
impose their combined will upon the vanquished and to subordinate
all interests to their own. . . .

55 It is useless to close our eyes to the fact that the power to
compel obedience by the exercise of the united strength of 'The
Five' is the fundamental principle of the League. Justice is
secondary. Might is primary.

The League as now constituted will be the prey of greed and
60 intrigue; and the law of unanimity in the Council, which may
offer a restraint, will be broken or render the organization
powerless. It is called upon to stamp as just what is unjust.

We have a treaty of peace, but it will not bring permanent peace
because it is founded on the shifting sands of self-interest.

Lansing's Memorandum dated 8 May 1919. Reproduced in
Robert Lansing, *The Peace Negotiations: A Personal Narrative*
(London, Constable & Co., 1921), pp 244–5

Questions

a   Explain (i) 'unctuous sophistry' (lines 13–14); (ii) 'sanctimonious
    pharisaism' (line 16).
b   Suggest why Nicolson felt that the peacemakers in 1919 'were
    very stupid men' (line 2).
c   From your knowledge of the peace treaties, do you agree that
    the final settlement was 'an Imperialistic peace' (lines 11–12)
    disguised 'under the surface of Wilsonism' (line 12)?
d   Comment on the last sentence of extract *a*.
e   What justification does the second extract provide for Harold
    Nicolson's opinion in extract *a*?

* *f* Suggest (i) which articles in the Treaty of Versailles could have appeared to Lansing 'impossible of performance' (line 29); (ii) which articles in the Peace treaties contained 'the seeds of war' (line 33). Explain clearly why.

  g Comment on Lansing's reference to the 'peoples . . . given to others' (lines 39–41).

* *h* Did Lansing's expectations prove correct in (i) the early postwar years; (ii) later years?

5 East and Central Europe: a democratic experiment

(a) Extracts from a Bolshevist leaflet, anonymous and undated, distributed in Vienna

Proletarians and soldiers: representatives of the Entente capitalists are daily humiliating the Government of Austrian exploiters. The robber league styling itself the Entente now wishes to dictate to us our fate. Look to the East. The Hungarian proletariat has
5 overthrown its exploiters and scattered its rapacious enemies in an impetuous assault. The Entente, internally shaken, is already offering peace to the invincible Hungarian proletariat . . . whereas it scorns and mocks at the German–Austrian proletariat because it still suffers itself to be led by the nose by a handful of bloodsuckers.
10 Comrades, if you wish to shake off the yoke of the Entente you must first of all destroy your own oppressors in order to set free your forces to fight the Entente capitalists. You will not remain alone. Troops of the Hungarian Army, filled with enthusiasm, are already at the frontier in order to hurry like brothers to your aid in
15 the class struggle.
Comrades, if you realize the dictatorship of the proletariat you will achieve the same result as your Hungarian brethren who draw three times as much pay and live in the palaces of the rich. If you proclaim the dictatorship of the proletariat the Hungarian Soviet
20 Republic will place at your disposal its immense granaries, newly filled by captures in Slovakia, since international class solidarity imposes on the Hungarian proletariat the duty to share its last crust with its Austrian brother. . . .

> Reproduced in Maxwell H. H. Macartney, *Five Years of European Chaos* (London, Chapman & Hall, 1923), pp 57–8

(b) An eminent economist, member of the British delegation at Versailles in 1919, views east and central Europe

[In Russia, Hungary and Austria] the miseries of life and the
25 disintegration of society are too notorious to require analysis; and these countries are already experiencing the actuality of what for

the rest of Europe is still in the realm of prediction. Yet they comprehend a vast territory and a great population, and are an extant example of how much man can suffer and how far society
30 can decay. Above all, they are the signal to us of how in the final catastrophe the malady of the body passes over into malady of the mind. Economic privation proceeds by easy stages, and so long as men suffer it patiently the outside world cares little. Physical efficiency and resistance to disease slowly diminish, but life
35 proceeds somehow, until the limit of human endurance is reached at last and counsels of despair and madness stir the sufferers from the lethargy which precedes the crisis. Then man shakes himself, and the bonds of custom are loosed. The power of ideas is sovereign, and he listens to whatever instruction of hope, illusion,
40 or revenge is carried to him on the air. As I write, the flames of Russian Bolshevism seem, for the moment at least, to have burnt themselves out, and the peoples of Central and Eastern Europe are held in a dreadful torpor. The lately gathered harvest keeps off the worst privations, and Peace has been declared at Paris. But winter
45 approaches. Men will have nothing to look forward to or to nourish hopes on. There will be little fuel to moderate the rigours of the season or to comfort the starved bodies of the town-dwellers.

But who can say how much is endurable, or in what direction
50 men will seek at last to escape from their misfortunes?

John Maynard Keynes, *The Economic Consequences of Peace* (London, Macmillan, 1920), pp 233–5

Questions

a Which points made in the 'Bolshevist leaflet', do you think, stand most in need of checking? Against which other sources would you test their reliability?

b Using internal evidence, suggest the probable date of the 'leaflet'.

c How effective do you consider the 'leaflet' to have been as a means of propagating Bolshevism?

d How can extract *b* be used to disprove the Bolshevist propaganda in the 'leaflet'?

e Explain and comment on Keynes' statement that 'these countries are already experiencing the actuality of what for the rest of Europe is still in the realm of prediction' (lines 26–7).

★ f 'But winter approaches' (lines 44–5). With close reference to Keynes' extract, say to what extent and in what ways seasonal conditions are a force of change in history.

6   The Thick Cloud of Mystery

(a) A note on secret diplomacy

After the experience of the last three months [January–March 1919] I am convinced that the method of personal interviews and private conclaves is a failure. It has given every opportunity for intrigue, plotting, bargaining, and combining. The President, as I
5   now see it, should have insisted on everything being brought before the Plenary Conference. He would then have had the confidence and support of all the smaller nations because they would have looked up to him as their champion and guide. They would have followed him.
10   The result of the present method has been to destroy their faith and arouse their resentment. They look upon the President as in favour of a world ruled by Five Great Powers, an international despotism of the strong, in which the little nations are merely rubber-stamps.
15   The President has undoubtedly found himself in a most difficult position. He has put himself on a level with politicians experienced in intrigue, whom he will find a pretty difficult lot. He will sink in the estimation of the delegates who are not within the inner circle, and what will be still more disastrous will be the loss of confidence
20   among the peoples of the nations represented here. A grievous blunder has been made.

(b) Memorandum on the Fiume Controversy, dated 29 March 1919

My fear is that the President will continue to rely upon private interviews and his powers of persuasion to induce the Italians to abandon their extravagant claim. I am sure that he will not be able
25   to do it. On the contrary, his conversations will strengthen rather than weaken Italian determination. He ought to tell them *now* that he will not consent to have Fiume given to Italy. It would cause anger and bitterness, but nothing to compare with the resentment which will be aroused if the uncertainty is permitted to go on
30   much longer. . . .
    The future is darkened by the Adriatic situation and I look to an explosion before the matter is settled. It is a good thing that the President visited Italy when he did and when blessings rather than curses greeted him. Secret diplomacy is reaping a new harvest of
35   execrations and condemnations. Will the practice ever cease?

> Both 'Note' and 'Memorandum' written by Robert Lansing, Woodrow Wilson's Secretary of State and member of the American Peace Commission in Paris, and reproduced in his *The Peace Negotiations: A Personal Narrative* (London, Constable & Co., 1921), pp 195–6, 206

   a Arrive at a definition of 'secret diplomacy' in the light of extract *a*. What evidence could Lansing have had in support of his claim that this 'method' was a 'failure'? Explain the historical context of Lansing's reference to (i) 'Plenary Conference' (line 6); (ii) 'smaller nations' (line 7).

★ *b* On what grounds were the Italians pressing for sovereignty over Fiume? Suggest reasons why President Wilson took a firm stand against Italy's claim.

★ *c* With particular reference to the Austrian Tyrol and the port of Danzig, how convincing, do you think, was the Italian claim?

★ *d* 'The most Italy could do [in 1919] was to hit the headlines, not raise the alarm' (Taylor). Discuss.

★ *e* To what extent, and for what reasons, may the Fiume controversy be described as the prelude to Fascism in Italy?

   f What impression of Woodrow Wilson do you get from the two extracts and how far does it compare with that formed from extract 3*a*?

7 Findings of a Postwar Diarist

(a) France's obsession with security

[Paris, Sunday, 6 March 1921] As for the French, they are as determined to exact reparation for all their fearful sufferings as the Germans are to evade it. We have 100,000 French and British troops in the Rhineland, and there are the Belgians and Americans
5 besides. We can spare but few more, as all our troops are either in Ireland or in the occupation of mandated territories or plebiscite areas. . . . The French seem ready for anything, but we know little of the real feeling of the French people, and I see already appeals to the communists and the proletariat of Europe to prevent
10 the sanctions. The French think that they can carry out the first moves without mobilising. No doubt they can, but what with incidents, troubles, strikes, and so forth the future is obscure, and I should prefer to shut down the German frontiers to all trade and trust to blockade rather than to military measures which may lead
15 the French to Berlin, if not to Moscow. But this may not be the French view. I feel sure that Foch's desire for the military frontier of the Rhine remains unchanged. The French are not convinced that Germany is adequately crushed and prevented from reviving. There is no real peace, only an enforced truce, and while we have
20 broken up our old friend Austria we have made Germany more united than ever. So one must regard the general prospect as grave, and while admitting constraint to be indispensible one need not approve of the pending methods of applying it. A blockade is

our most effective instrument, and it is better to take this course
than to start out unconsciously on the road to Berlin.

(b) A conversation with 'Le Temps' correspondent

[Paris, Tuesday, 8 March 1921] M. Herbette, who writes the
leaders on foreign policy in *Le Temps*, came and had a good talk.
We think that the occupation will do no good, but that the
customs duties may if generally applied, and we preferred that
they should be applied all round Germany, and not upon one
fraction of one frontier. Like Pétain, he favoured remaining till the
Boches paid.

I told him of my projected trip to Vienna, etc. I got out the map
of post-war Europe and told him that I could find no policy in
London on all this question. I wanted him to give me the French
policy, or at least his own. He thought, like Pétain, that we had
made a bad peace, and regretted the break-up of Austria as I did.
Czecho-Slovakia now stretched across Europe and was like a
cartridge of dynamite, hating every body round them, but
appearing to him more Slav and pro-Russian than anything else.
Austria was bound to go to Germany some day, and Germany
would then extend over Hungary next. He thought the new Serb
State had more possibilities than any other carved out of the old
Austria. We agreed to differ about the Greeks. He thought that we
were laying up great trouble for ourselves in future with Russia,
owing to our backing of the Greeks and because of the little Baltic
States which we had created. A revived Russia would sweep all
this away. He was critical and suspicious of L[loyd] G[eorge] and
was sarcastic about the manoeuvring in London last Sunday.
Briand would certainly have been upset had the Boches accepted
L[loyd] G[eorge]'s compromise, but fortunately they refused the
terms. They were our wisest counsellors, said M. Herbette.

> Lieut-Col C. à Court Repington CMG, *After the War: A
> Diary* (London, Constable & Co., 1922), pp 71–2, 74

Questions

a   Explain the author's reference, in extract *a*, to (i) Ireland (line
6); (ii) 'mandated territories' (line 6); (iii) 'plebiscite areas' (lines
6–7); (iv) 'Foch's desire for the military frontier of the Rhine'
(lines 16–17).

★ b   'France's obsession with security is historically understandable
and justified.' Discuss.

★ c   The break-up of Austria 'made Germany more united than
ever' (lines 20–1). How valid is this statement?

d   Comment on the last sentence of extract *a*.

e   Explain 'not upon one fraction of one frontier' (lines 30–1), and identify (i) Pétain (line 31); (ii) the Boches (line 32); (iii) Briand (line 50).

  ★ *f* From your knowledge of the period, analyse critically Herbette's views on (i) Czechoslovakia; (ii) Austria; (iii) Germany; (iv) the Greeks.

     g Explain the historical background to the last three sentences in extract *b*: 'He was critical . . . wisest counsellors' (lines 48–52).

8   Franco–Polish Agreement, 19 February 1921

The Polish Government and the French Government, both desirous of safeguarding, by the maintenance of the Treaties both have signed or which may in future be recognized by both Parties, the peace of Europe, the security of their territories, and their
5 common political and economic interests, have agreed as follows:

(i) In order to coordinate their endeavours toward peace the two Governments undertake to consult each other on all questions of foreign policy which concern both States, so far as those questions affect the settlement of international relations in the spirit of the
10 Treaties and in accordance with the Covenant of the League of Nations.

(ii) In view of the fact that economic restoration is the essential preliminary condition of the re-establishment of international order and peace in Europe, the two Governments shall come to an
15 understanding in this regard with a view to concerted action and mutual support.

They will endeavour to develop their economic relations, and for this purpose will conclude special agreements and a Commercial Treaty.
20 (iii) If, notwithstanding the sincerely peaceful views and intentions of the two contracting States, either or both of them should be attacked without provocation, the two Governments shall take concerted measures for the defence of their territory and the protection of their legitimate interests within the limits
25 specified in the Preamble.

(iv) The two Governments undertake to consult each other before concluding new agreements which will affect their policy in central and eastern Europe.

(v) The present Agreement shall not come into force until the
30 commercial agreements now in course of negotiation have been signed.

Paris, 19 February 1921.

                         Aristide Briand
                         E. Sapieha

Le livre jaune Français: Documents diplomatiques (1938–1939) (Paris, Imprimerie nationale, 1939), Appendix 1, trans. D. Thomson

Questions

★ *a* Explain the historical circumstances leading up to the Franco–Polish Agreement in 1921.

b 'Poland cannot stand unless the Allies support her. A Russo–German combination is certain eventually if the Allies do not cultivate a strong Poland.' Discuss the significance of the Agreement in the light of this quotation.

★ *c* 'The political agreement between France and Poland reached at Paris on February 19, 1921, set the tone and model for a series of treaties with eastern European states . . . made between 1924 and 1927.' Explain fully.

9   The March on Rome, October 1922

(a) Proclamation by the Quadrumvirate, 26 October 1922

Fascisti! Italians! The time for determined battle has come! Four years ago the National Army loosed at this season the final offensive, which brought it to victory. Today the army of the Black-shirts takes again possession of that victory, which has been
5 mutilated, and going directly to Rome brings victory again to the glory of that capital. From now on *principi* and *triari* are mobilized. The martial law of Fascism now becomes a fact. By order of the Duce all the military, political, and administrative functions of the party management are taken over by a secret Quadrumvirate of
10 Action with dictatorial powers.

The Army, the reserve and safeguard of the Nation, must not take part in the struggle. Fascism renews its highest homage given to the Army of Vittorio Veneto. Fascism, furthermore, does not march against the police, but against a political class both cowardly
15 and imbecile, which in four long years has not been able to give a Government to the nation. Those who form the productive class must know that Fascism wants to impose nothing more than order and discipline upon the nation and to help to raise the strength which will renew progress and prosperity. The people
20 who work in the fields and in the factories, those who work on the railroads or in offices, have nothing to fear from the Fascist Government. Their just rights will be protected. We will even be generous with unarmed adversaries.

Fascism draws its sword to cut the multiple Gordian knots
25 which tie and burden Italian life. We call God and the spirit of our five hundred thousand dead to witness that only one impulse sends us on, that only one passion burns within us – the impulse and the passion to contribute to the safety and greatness of our country.

30   Fascisti of all Italy! Stretch forth like Romans your spirits and your fibres! We must win! We will!

> Benito Mussolini, *My Autobiography* (London, Hutchinson, revised edition, 1939), pp 167–8

(b) A historian's view

[Vittorio Emanuele's] decision [on 28 October 1922] converted the fascists from outlaws into indispensible members of the next government. When Facta resigned, Salandra was invited to
35 become prime minister and he asked Mussolini to join the new administration; but the latter refused, on the assumption that he could now name his own price. Salandra thereupon withdrew and, fearing that the choice might otherwise be Giolitti, advised the king to appoint Mussolini – a man who was leading an armed
40 rebellion against the state and whose private army was responsible for countless atrocities throughout Italy. On 29 October, the king accepted this advice and Mussolini, at the age of only thirty-nine, became the twenty-seventh prime minister of Italy.

But the fascist leader was not satisfied with something so
45 unspectacular as a royal appointment. He needed to develop the myth of a march on Rome by 300,000 armed fascists to enforce an 'ultimatum' he had given to the king, and eventually a legend was invented of Mussolini on horseback leading his legions across the Rubicon. . . . [T]he myth was launched of fascism winning power
50 by an armed insurrection after a civil war and the loss of 3,000 men. These fictitious 3,000 'fascist martyrs' soon took their place in the government-sponsored history books. . . .

The absence of resistance implies that the public lacked confidence in the liberal leaders and was ready to accept the new
55 government with resignation, if not pleasure. Fear of communism can have been only a minor motive as there was no communist threat. A much more realistic fear was felt by those among the wealthy who were concerned lest Giolitti return to power with a policy of high taxes and social reform. Still more widespread was
60 the feeling that fascism was an alternative to anarchy – the last resort, as it were, after parliament had failed to function in defence of law and order; few were troubled by the fact that the anarchy had been deliberately fanned by fascism itself.

> Denis Mack Smith, *Mussolini* (London, Granada, 1983), pp 63–5

Questions

a   'Fascism was the shadow or ugly child of Communism' (Churchill). What (i) similarities and (ii) differences can you discern between fascism and communism from a close reading of the Quadrumvirate Proclamation and extracts 3b and 5a?

b Identify Vittorio Emanuele's 'decision' (line 32). How did this decision convert 'the fascists from outlaws into indispensible members of the next government' (lines 32–4)?
★ *c* Explain the historical connotations of the 'legend' (line 47). Suggest reasons why Mussolini felt that 'the myth of a march on Rome' (lines 45–6) was a political expedient.
d Who is Giolitti (line 38)?
★ *e* If it was neither communism nor political anarchy, what did, in fact, favour the rise of fascism to power in Italy?
★ *f* The 'march' on Rome 'occurred *after* and not before Mussolini's assumption of the premiership. There never in fact was a "seizure" of power . . . only a *threat* to seize power' (Grenville). Discuss.

10   The Occupation of the Ruhr, 11 January 1923

(a) *The Reich President, Friedrich Ebert, reaffirms German unity, during his visit to Karlsruhe immediately after the French irruption into Baden*

The blow which has been dealt us here is aimed at the greatest thing which we have saved from the war and the collapse, it is aimed at the unity of the Reich; this blow – we are convinced – will also be parried by the firm will and resolute loyalty of the
5   Baden people. The days when one could separate north and south in Germany are gone for ever; every German has now the unshatterable consciousness that he is the son of a single people and the member of a single Reich; no foreign violence will ever separate what race, speech and culture have knit together in the
10 course of an eventful history. Every German is aware to-day of the seriousness of the hour; every one of us knows that the future of the Reich, the very existence of the German Republic, is at stake. If in these fateful days we collect all our strength, we will repulse also all the attacks upon our national existence. By this
15 resolute and determined resistance we hope and expect that, in spite of everything, we shall achieve a better future for our hardly-proved people in the consciousness of our solidarity and our right, in the struggle for our freedom.

> Reproduced in Maxwell H. H. Macartney, *Five Years of European Chaos* (London, Chapman & Hall, 1923), pp 157–8

(b) *A contemporary scholar's view*

The great disservice which France has done not only to herself but
20 to all Europe has been the occupation with Belgium of the Ruhr.

The threat of the occupation was a most valuable trump-card so long as it was unplayed; played, it has essentially weakened France's position and prestige and . . . has had the very disconcerting effect of re-uniting Germany to a degree unknown
25 since the first few weeks of the war. The strong probability of this development ought to have been foreseen by all students of Germany history since the Armistice. But the gradual moral recuperation of the German people appears to have been but faintly appreciated in a France which seemed to be even more
30 afraid of her conquered enemy than she had been of the Germany of 1914, and which, disregarding the moral factors, was concentrating her attention upon the purely material resources of the foe and was falling into constant hysterics every time that the officers of General Nollet's Mission discovered a pickelhaube or a
35 fowling-piece on the farmstead of some Prussian or Bavarian Junker. The consequence was that the French, when they came seriously to push forward their so-called historical 'Rhine Policy', made three capital miscalculations.

In the first place . . . the French . . . evidently decided that the
40 defeat of 1918 was enough to obliterate the forty years of greatness to which Bismarck's genius had brought the country. . . .

The second great mistake of the French consisted in the false belief that they had a contribution to make to German culture.
. . . They have [however] burst into Germany with empty hands,
45 wrote . . . Professor Hermann Oncken, and 'they have nothing to offer us, and can no longer entice us aside by any means. Politically, economically, socially, technically, even culturally they represent an older and superseded type.' . . .

Finally . . . the third fundamental error of the French has been
50 in trying to wage this economic war of conquest with old-fashioned weapons.
Ibid., pp 11–13

(c) A historian's view

The occupation of the Ruhr gave the final touch to the deterioration of the mark. By 1 July 1923 the rate of exchange with the dollar had risen to a hundred and sixty thousand marks; by 1 August to a
55 million; by 1 November to a hundred and thirty thousand million. The collapse of the currency not only meant the end of trade, bankrupt businesses, food shortage in the big cities and unemployment: it had the effect, which is the unique quality of economic catastrophe, of reaching down to and touching every
60 single member of the community in a way which no political event can. The savings of the middle classes and working classes were wiped out at a single blow with a ruthlessness which no revolution could ever equal; at the same time the purchasing

power of wages was reduced to nothing. Even if a man worked
65   till he dropped it was impossible to buy enough clothes for his
family – and work, in any case, was not to be found.

    Whatever the cause of this phenomenon . . . the result of the
inflation was to undermine the foundations of German society in a
way which neither the war, nor the revolution of November
70   1918, nor the Treaty of Versailles had ever done. The real
revolution in Germany was the inflation, for it destroyed not only
property and money, but faith in property and the meaning of
money. The violence of Hitler's denunciations of the corrupt,
Jew-ridden system which had allowed all this to happen, the
75   bitterness of his attacks on the Versailles settlement and on the
Republican Government which had accepted it, found an echo in
the misery and despair of large classes of the German nation.

      Alan Bullock, *Hitler: A Study in Tyranny* (Harmondsworth,
    Penguin, second edition, 1962), pp 90–1

Questions

a   'All the questions pending between the Allies and Germany
were largely psychologic[al]' (Edward Beneš). Discuss with
close reference to extracts *a* and *b*.

b   Explain and comment on each of France's 'three capital
miscalculations' mentioned in extract *b*.

c   'The year 1923–4 marked France's last effort to attain what she
had failed to secure at Versailles, a means of checking the
future threat of German preponderance in Europe' (Grenville).
Do you agree?

★ d   The occupation of the Ruhr 'separated [France] from Britain
. . . and [the Germans] exploited the split successfully in the
1920s' (Grenville). Discuss.

e   'The real revolution in Germany was the inflation' (lines 70–1).
How valid, do you think, Bullock's verdict is?

★ f   Do you agree with A. J. P. Taylor that 'the occupation of the
Ruhr provided, in the long run, the strongest argument in
favour of appeasement'?

II A Reign of Illusions 1924–29

Introduction

The years between the Ruhr crisis and the onset of the economic crisis constituted a period of optimism and 'fulfilment', promising a 'future' which, according to President Hoover, gleamed 'bright with hope', and marking what appeared to be then a process of 'pacification by pact'. The League of Nations had gradually begun to establish its authority and to gain prestige and influence. It was generally recognised as a constructive force of peace and security in Europe. The 'many political and economic problems' were approached with great diplomatic finesse. Negotiation was a healthy substitute for confrontation. The Locarno Treaties provide the student of the period with tangible evidence of this spirit of international cooperation and stability. A year before Locarno, the Dawes Plan had helped the Weimar Republic honour her reparation commitments through the provision of American loans – an encouraging sign that the United States, which had previously declined membership of the League, was getting 'involuntarily' involved in European affairs. In 1926 Germany joined the League and was accorded a permanent seat on the Council. 'In Europe,' observes Gathorne-Hardy, the year of Locarno 'marks definitely the conclusion of a period of preliminary settlement, and the start of a "policy of fulfilment" which promised at least a temporary stability.' The hopeful prospects of disarmament received broader dimensions by general declarations 'to outlaw' war as 'an instrument of national policy'.

The mood and spirit of these years owed much to the outlook and personality of each of the three highly influential ministers responsible for the foreign policy of France, Britain and Weimar Germany: Aristide Briand, Austen Chamberlain and Gustav Stresemann. Collectively, these advocates of reconciliation 'established a remarkable degree of mutual confidence and friendship which in itself helped to stabilise European affairs', fusing 'their national policies into a general policy of pacification' (Thomson). On the other hand, both Fascist Italy and Stalinist Russia were still adopting a cautious attitude to international affairs, while National Socialism in Germany was not yet in a position to challenge the peace and territorial settlement of 1919.

These conditions, which made *rapprochement* in Europe possible, disappeared in 1929. In May Chamberlain lost office. Stresemann, 'the cynical old roué who had given his last years to the noblest of illusions' (Cobban) died in October. In November the farseeing Briand was replaced by the undiplomatic André Tardieu. These months witnessed the catastrophic crash on Wall Street, plunging the United States, Europe and the world into the Great Depression. France, whose national security was still being traditionally and consistently based on the illusive belief in allied support, began the building of the great Maginot Line along the entire length of the Franco–German border. It was symptomatic of the fast-changing political circumstances. Overall disarmament had developed into an exercise of wishful thinking. Within the next year there were strong indications of a steady revival of German nationalism.

Were not all the international pacts and treaties and conferences, envisaged to guarantee 'collective security', a subconscious admission that the League of Nations was not in fact an effective institution? The lull of these years of peace and stability was over. The war had been a tremendous force of change and it was already becoming evident at this stage that society – in all its cultural manifestations – was feeling the necessity to re-examine all its 'traditional ideas about reality, all values, all principles' (K. Mannheim).

1   The Dawes Plan, 1924

(a) The Committee of Experts' Report

We have approached our task as business men anxious to obtain effective results. We have been concerned with the technical, and not the political, aspects of the problem presented to us. . . . Questions of military occupation are also not within our terms of
5   reference. . . . [O]ur forecasts are based on the assumption [however] that economic activity will be unhampered and unaffected by any foreign organization other than the controls herein provided. Consequently, our plan is based upon the assumption that existing measures, in so far as they hamper that
10 activity, will be withdrawn or sufficiently modified as soon as Germany has put into execution the plan recommended, and that they will not be re-imposed except in the case of flagrant failure to fulfil the conditions accepted by common agreement. . . .

The task would be hopeless if the present situation of Germany
15 accurately reflected her potential capacity; the proceeds from Germany's national production could not in that case enable her both to meet her national needs and to ensure the payment of her foreign debts.

But Germany's growing and industrious population; her great
technical skill; the wealth of her material resources; the development
of her agriculture on progressive lines; her eminence in industrial
science; all these factors enable us to be hopeful with regard to her
future production.

Further, ever since 1919 the country has been improving its
plant and equipment; the experts specially appointed to examine
the railways have shown in their report that expense has not been
spared in improving the German railway system; telephone and
telegraph communications have been assured with the help of the
most modern appliances; harbours and canals have likewise been
developed; lastly, the industrialists have been enabled further to
increase an entirely modern plant which is now adapted in many
industries to produce a greater output than before the war.

Germany is therefore well equipped with resources; she possesses
the means for exploiting them on a large scale; when the present
credit shortage has been overcome, she will be able to resume a
favoured position in the activity of a world where normal
conditions of exchange are gradually being restored.

Without undue optimism, it may be anticipated that Germany's
production will enable her to satisfy her own requirements and
raise the amounts contemplated in this plan for reparation
obligations.

> *Documents of European Economic History*, vol iii, *The End of
> Old Europe 1914–1939*, eds Sidney Pollard and Colin
> Holmes (London, Edward Arnold, 1973), pp 294–5

(b) A historian's view

What were the main characteristics of the [Dawes] Plan which was
finally worked out by the experts, and accepted by the interested
governments in April 1924?

Unlike the missions originally set up by the different committees,
this plan was concerned entirely with a new settlement of the
problem of reparations. This settlement, according to the total of
the first annuities provided for, implicitly entailed a further
reduction of the total debt. Obviously this meant new concessions
by France.

What France obtained in return, however, was decisive. The
German payments were henceforth guaranteed by pledges,
established by the experts, recognized by all creditors and accepted
by Germany: mortgages on the German railways and industry,
deductions from various German taxes. There would be established
in Berlin an international commission responsible for the
supervision of German currency, a railways commissioner, a
commissioner for revenue from the Reich, and a general agent for
reparations, the American Parker Gilbert, upon whom fell from

60 then on the responsibility for solving the problem of transfers. By this compromise France exchanged her freedom of action with regard to Germany and her illusions regarding the magnitude of what she could expect to receive, for the certainty of being paid to a certain extent.

> J. Néré, *The Foreign Policy of France from 1914 to 1945* (London, Routledge & Kegan Paul, 1975), pp 57–8

Questions

a Identify and comment briefly on the historical significance of (i) 'the problem presented to us' (line 3); (ii) 'existing measures' (line 9); (iii) 'the present credit shortage' (lines 34–5); (iv) 'the interested governments' (lines 43–4).

b Why were 'reparation obligations' (lines 40–1) a key issue in 1924?

★ c What were the recommendations of the Committee of Experts? How did the Dawes Plan contribute to the general stability of the mid and later 1920s?

d '[S]uch heavy and entirely unproductive obligations as those to which Germany was subjected under the Dawes Plan' (Hitler). In the light of this quotation from *Mein Kampf* and of extract *b*, what criticism can be made of the Dawes Plan from the German point of view?

e 'Germany is therefore well-equipped with resources' (line 33). Summarise briefly what extract *a* tells us about Germany's 'potential capacity' (line 15).

★ f 'Obviously this meant new concessions by France' (lines 49–50). What *other* concessions did France have to make between 1919 and 1924? Say briefly why.

★ g How 'decisive' (line 51) were France's gains from her acceptance of the Dawes Plan?

2 The Locarno Agreement

(a) Treaty of Mutual Guarantee between Germany, Belgium, France, Great Britain and Italy, 16 October 1925

1. The High Contracting Parties collectively and severally guarantee, in the manner provided in the following articles, the maintenance of the territorial *status quo* resulting from the frontiers between Germany and Belgium and between Germany and France
5 and the inviolability of the said frontiers as fixed by or in pursuance of the Treaty of Peace signed at Versailles on the 28th June, 1919 and also the observance of the stipulations of Articles 42 and 43 of the said treaty concerning the demilitarized zone.

2. Germany and Belgium, and also Germany and France, mutually
10 undertake that they will in no case attack or invade each other or resort to war against each other.

This stipulation shall not, however, apply in the case of –

1. The exercise of the right of legitimate defence, that is to say, resistance to a violation of the undertaking contained in the previous paragraph or to a flagrant breach of Articles 42 or 43 of the said Treaty of Versailles, if such breach constitutes an unprovoked act of aggression and by reason of the assembly of armed forces in the demilitarized zone immediate action is necessary. . . .

3. In view of the undertakings entered into in Article 2 . . ., Germany and Belgium and Germany and France undertake to settle by peaceful means . . . all questions of every kind which may arise between them and which it may not be possible to settle by the normal methods of diplomacy . . .

4. 1. If one of the High Contracting Parties alleges that a violation of Article 2 of the present Treaty or a breach of Articles 42 or 43 of the Treaty of Versailles has been or is being committed, it shall bring the question at once before the Council of the League of Nations.

2. As soon as the Council of the League of Nations is satisfied that such violation or breach has been committed, it will notify its finding without delay to the Powers signatory of the present Treaty, who severally agree that in such case they will each of them come immediately to the assistance of the Power against whom the act complained of is directed.

3. In case of a flagrant violation . . . by one of the High Contracting Parties, each of the other Contracting Parties hereby undertakes immediately to come to the help of the party against whom such a violation or breach has been directed . . . .

League of Nations Treaty Series, vol liv (1926–7), pp 291–7

(b) Aristide Briand on the origin and justification of Locarno. Speech delivered before the Chamber of Deputies, 25 February 1926

What struck me at the time of the discussion of the Treaty of Versailles . . . was the tragic dialogue which was carried on between different members of the Chamber at that time, over the pressing concern to guarantee the security of France.

This was indeed the thought which dominated the whole assembly. The material conditions of the Treaty, although they were important, were a secondary consideration. We were emerging from a hideous war, and we had only one idea: to avoid another war, and the whole discussion centred on this point. This was the dialogue that I heard:

Are we certain that the clause of the Treaty in which we renounce the guarantee of a natural frontier, the clause which promises us the combined guarantee of the USA and Britain, will work? . . .

When one speaker added, 'But if the Treaty is not ratified by
the USA, what will become of the British guarantee?', M
Clemenceau replied, 'I hope that the British guarantee will work.'

When someone insisted again, saying, 'This British guarantee is
bound up with the American guarantee; it is an integral part of it,
and if the latter country fails, and Britain consequently considers
herself free, what will happen then?', I can still see M Clemenceau
raising his hands and murmuring, 'Well, then, there will be no
longer a Treaty; there will be nothing.'

Well! gentlemen, when chance circumstances brought me to
power in 1921, I considered that my first duty was to use all
my strength, all my mind and all my heart, to try to fill in this
gap. . . .

At the Cannes Conference . . . discussions continued on this
subject with representatives of the British government. Their
outcome was favourable. . . . It was agreed that the British
guarantee would be given. . . .

At the same time, gentlemen, the notion of the Geneva protocol
was born in Cannes. There the organization of the Genoa
Conference for the whole of Europe was being prepared, in which
no nation could participate without previously signing a non-
aggression pact. Hence we thought that we could bring to the
nations of Europe a whole vast system of peace, a whole vast plan
of international organization.

Was it a matter of an ordinary alliance, similar to all the others
between Britain and France? No, gentlemen! And you will find in
the Blue Book, which the British government published at the
time, a record of discussions during which it had been perfectly
understood that, when a guarantee agreement had been made
between Britain and France, Germany could, and even must,
enter.

Gentlemen, this is the very essence of the Locarno Treaty.
When the worthy M Herriot had the reparations plan with which
you are acquainted accepted in London, the question of an
understanding between the peoples of Europe was naturally again
put forward to carry out this plan.

It was then that the suggestion of Mr Stresemann, that is, the
suggestion of the German government, originated. I seized upon
this suggestion. In it I found again the thought that I had had at
Cannes. I considered that the events which had taken place since
1921 were such as to strengthen in my mind the wish to form a
new agreement whose necessity had become apparent to me, and I
gave this my greatest attention.

Reproduced in J. Néré, op cit, pp 283–4

Questions

a   Identify Articles 42 and 43 of the Treaty of Versailles (lines 7–8, 15, 26).

b   Comment briefly on the circumstances which necessitated the Locarno Agreement in 1925.

★ c   What agreements, other than that in extract *a*, were reached by the 'High Contracting Parties' at Locarno in 1925?

d   Who is Aristide Briand? Explain the historical significance of 'when chance circumstances brought me to power in 1921' (lines 63–4).

e   Identify 'the Cannes Conference' (line 67) and explain what is meant by 'the notion of the Geneva protocol' (line 71). What was the purpose of 'the Genoa Conference' (lines 72–3)?

f   '[T]his is the very essence of the Locarno Treaty' (line 85). Summarise and briefly explain 'the origin and justification' of the Locarno Treaty as set out by Aristide Briand in extract *b*.

★ g   How did the Weimar Republic profit from the Locarno Agreement?

★ h   'Locarno marked another stage in French disillusionment as well as in that of its East European allies' (Hiden). What criticism can be made of Briand's speech in extract *b* in the light of this quotation?

3   Germany: a force for peace in Europe?

(a) Germany joins the League

Berlin, 10 January 1926 – Another step forward. Germany has decided to send in her application for admission to the League of Nations. The debate in the Reichstag on this subject revealed considerable opposition, notably from Bavaria. It is said that even
5   Hindenburg, who has proved an admirable President, is against joining the League now; he is believed to be in favour of waiting at least until September. The idea of those who advocate this course is that, by waiting a little longer, Germany can obtain larger countervalues for entering the League. I rejoin that once
10 Germany is a member of the League she will be able to make her voice heard better than before, and that no counterconcessions can be expected for doing what is so much in Germany's own interest. . . .
Berlin, 2 October 1926 – Now that Locarno has been in force for
15 nearly a year, and that Germany is a member of the League of Nations, a definite period in history comes to a close. A fresh epoch for Europe commences, and the work here will assume a different and more normal character. The war spirit has been quelled, and the possibility of an era of peaceful development
20 opens. . . .

During the years 1925–26 the German Ministers in charge of affairs have accomplished what even Bismarck and the post-Bismarckians attempted in vain. . . .

The outcome of events during the last two years had been this, that the object aimed at by former German statesmen has now been achieved by novel means in widely different – perhaps more difficult – circumstances. For it may be confidently said that the animosity between England and Germany has been in large measure appeased, the proof being that England is now brought in as an arbitrator, and as a guarantor of the territorial integrity, not only of France, but also of Germany. Moreover, it is mainly through English influence that Germany has obtained at Geneva a position acceptable to her national dignity.

Edgar Vincent D'Abernon, *An Ambassador of Peace: Pages from the Diary of Viscount D'Abernon* (London, A. P. Watt & Son, 1929–30). Reproduced in *Germany from Empire to Ruin, 1913–1945*, ed. Henry Cord Meyer (London, Macmillan, 1973), pp 144–5, 146.

Viscount D'Abernon was the British ambassador to Berlin between 1920 and 1926

(b) Stresemann on the meaning of 'parliamentary system'. Speech delivered to the Executive Committee of the Deutsche Volkspartei, 26 February 1928

Let us not fool ourselves about this: we are in the midst of a parliamentary crisis that is already more than a crisis of conscience. This crisis has two roots: one the caricature that has become of the parliamentary system in Germany, secondly the completely false position of parliament in relation to its responsibility to the nation.

What does 'parliamentary system' mean? It means the responsibility of the Reich minister to parliament, which can pass a vote of no confidence and force him to resign. In no way does it entail the allocation of ministerial offices according to the strength of the parliamentary parties. In no way does it entail the transference of government from the cabinet to the parliamentary parties. The minister is designated by the Reich President. It is clear that the President must take into account that ministers named by him secure the support of the majority of the Reichstag. Moreover, the appointment and dismissal of ministers is a question of their personal responsibility. I personally guard against the adoption of the idea that a parliamentary party 'withdraws' its minister. The ministers have to ask themselves whether they will accept office or give it up. The Reichstag can withdraw its confidence from them. The parliamentary party can exclude them from its membership but 'withdrawing' a minister means in reality that the individual ceases to exist and becomes a mere agent of one or another organisation. This conception means the end of liberalism in general. When we no longer have any liberal parties who can put up with the individual then they will cease to be bearers of liberalism.

> *Ursachen und Folgen. Vom deutschen Zusammenbruch 1918 und 1945 bis zur staatlichen Neuordnung Deutschlands in der Gegenwart*, eds H. Michaelis *et al* (Berlin, Dokumentation-Verlag, 1958), vol vii, pp 236–7. Reproduced in J. W. Hiden, *The Weimar Republic*, Seminar Studies in History (London, Longman, 1974), p 99

Questions

a   Suggest reasons why Hindenburg was 'against joining the League' (lines 5–6) in January 1926? What 'larger countervalues' (line 9) did those who, like Hindenburg, were in favour of delaying Germany's entry into the League, hope to obtain?

★ b   'The war spirit has been quelled' (lines 18–19). From your knowledge of the period, what evidence was there in the Europe of October 1926 that augured 'an era of peaceful development' (line 19)?

c   In the light of the third paragraph (extract *a*), explain and briefly comment on the historical significance of the author's claim that 'The outcome . . . circumstances.' (lines 24–7).

d   Identify the grave 'parliamentary crisis' referred to in the first paragraph of extract *b*.

e   Do you find Stresemann's definition of 'parliamentary system' given in lines 39–59 satisfactory?

★ f   What chances of survival, in your opinion, did the Weimar Republic have at this stage?

★ g   'If Germany had entered the League of Nations in 1921 or 1922, it is conceivable that this might have strengthened the few weak elements in Germany which were working for a peaceful co-operation in an organized world. But by 1926, the forces set upon revenge and Pan-Germanism had already regained far too much of a hold on the body politic' (Sumner Welles). In the light of this quotation, and with reference to the two extracts, to what extent was the Germany of October 1926 a true 'force for peace in Europe'?

4   Berlin in 1926: Leon Trotsky's impression

In the years before the war I had known Hohenzollern Berlin very well. It had then its own peculiar physiognomy, which no one could call pleasant but which many thought imposing. Berlin has changed. It has now no physiognomy at all, at least none that I
5   could discover. The city was slowly recovering from a long and

serious disease whose course had been accompanied by many surgical operations. The inflation was already over, but the stabilized mark served only as a means of measuring the general anaemia. In the streets, in the shops, on the faces of the pedestrians,
10 one sensed the impoverishment and also that impatient, often avid, desire to rise again. The German thoroughness and cleanliness during the hard years of war, of the defeat and the Versailles brigandage, had been swallowed up by dire poverty. The human ant-hill was stubbornly but joylessly restoring the passages,
15 corridors, and store-rooms crushed by the boot of war. In the rhythm of the streets, in the movements and gestures of the passers-by, one felt a tragic undercurrent of fatalism: 'Can't be helped; life is an indefinite term at hard-labour; we must begin again at the beginning.'

> Leon Trotsky, *My Life: An Attempt at an Autobiography*
> (Harmondsworth, Penguin, reprint, 1984), pp 545–6

Questions

a Who is Leon Trotsky?
b Suggest what Trotsky had in mind when he says 'The city was slowly recovering from a long and serious disease whose course had been accompanied by many surgical operations.' (lines 5–7).
c 'Berlin has changed' (lines 3–4). Do you think this autobiographical extract is an unbiased reflection of what Trotsky considers to have been a radical change for the worse in Berlin? What other sources would you consult to support your arguments?
★ d How and for what reasons are personal impressions such as Trotsky's useful to the historian of this period?

5 The Pact of Paris, August 1928

(a) Declaration of Principles

1. The High Contracting Parties solemnly declare in the names of their respective peoples that they condemn recourse to war for the solution of international controversies, and renounce it as an instrument of national policy in relations with one another.
5 2. The High Contracting Parties agree that the settlement or solution of all disputes or conflicts of whatever nature or of whatever origin they may be, which may arise among them, shall never be sought except by pacific means.
3. . . . This Treaty shall . . . remain open as long as may be
10 necessary for adherence by all the other Powers of the world.

> *League of Nations Treaty Series*, vol xciv (1929), pp 59–64

(b) A monument to illusion?

The [American] Senate had few illusions about the agreement for abolishing war. Senator Reed of Missouri branded it an 'international kiss,' while Senator Glass of Virginia did not want people to think him 'simple enough to suppose that it is worth a
15 postage stamp'. No formal reservations were attached to the treaty, but the Senate Foreign Relations committee did present an 'interpretation' reserving the right of self-defense, the right to fight for the Monroe Doctrine, and the right not to enforce the treaty against violators.

20   Such was the tidal wave of public opinion that the Senate approved the Kellogg–Briand Pact, in January, 1929, by a vote of 85 to 1. The next order of business was the bill for constructing fifteen new cruisers, which shortly thereafter were approved. The *New York Evening Post* jibed, 'If, after just having signed a peace
25 treaty with twenty-six nations, we need fifteen new cruisers, how many would we have needed if we hadn't just signed a peace treaty with twenty-six nations?'

   The Kellogg–Briand Pact proved to be a monument to illusion. It was not only delusive but dangerous, for it further lulled the
30 public, already prepared to lag behind in the naval race, into a false sense of security. Instead of outlawing wars, the treaty merely outlawed declarations of wars. Nations thereafter, always fighting defensively of course, tended to become involved in 'incidents', not wars.

> Thomas A. Bailey, *A Diplomatic History of the American People* (New Jersey, Prentice-Hall, tenth edition, 1980), p 650

Questions

a Who were the original 'High Contracting Parties' referred to in extract *a*?

b Explain briefly in your own words the 'principles' underlying the Pact of Paris. What importance would you attach to it as a historical event?

★ c What criticism of the Pact would you offer?

d In what ways does extract *b* reveal the American attitude towards European affairs during this period?

★ e '[A] monument to illusion' (line 28). How far are the doubts of the author of extract *b* justified?

6 The Economic Boom of the Later 1920s

(a) Indices of industrial production for selected regions, 1925–9 (1925 = 100)

	1925	1926	1927	1928	1929
Industrial Europe*	100	95.6	113.2	116.5	123.1
Agricultural Europe†	100	105.6	112.2	113.3	122.2
United States	100	106.0	105.0	110.0	123.0
Canada	100	113.8	121.5	133.8	143.0
U.S.S.R.	100	143.8	168.4	205.3	256.1
Rest of World‡	100	107.7	108.8	113.2	119.8
World Total§	100	102.2	108.7	113.0	120.7

* Austria, Belgium, U.K., Czechoslovakia, Denmark, France, Germany, Luxemburg, Netherlands, Sweden, Switzerland, and the Saar.

† Bulgaria, Estonia, Finland, Greece, Hungary, Italy, Latvia, Poland, Portugal, Romania, Spain, Yugoslavia.

‡ Includes ten countries in Latin America, Africa, Asia and Oceania: Argentina, Australia, Brazil, British India, Chile, Japan, Mexico, New Zealand, Peru, South Africa.

§ The world indices are probably on the low side since the League of Nations' estimates for the United States require some upward revision.

Sources: League of Nations, *World Production and Prices, 1925–1932* (1933), pp 45, 49; for the United States, O[rganization for] E[uropean] E[conomic] C[ooperation], *Industrial Statistics, 1900–1959* (Paris, 1960), p 9.

Derek H. Aldcroft, *From Versailles to Wall Street 1919–1929* (London, Allen Lane, 1977), p 188

(b) A historian's comment

The prosperity of the 1920s was real: production, trade, and personal incomes were undoubtedly growing. There was more real wealth in the world, per head of population in 1925, than there had been in 1913; and still more in 1929 than in 1925. But this wealth was more unevenly distributed, and there were now more people than before unable to share in the prosperity. There was a larger number of workers unemployed in most European countries – seldom below an average annual rate of ten per cent in the United Kingdom in these years. There were the primary producers of the world, able to supply more of some things than the manufacturing areas wanted or than others could afford, with the result that unsold stocks of wheat, sugar, and coffee accumulated. Various devices to increase or forestall purchasing power came into general use; chief among them the device of hire-purchase or deferred payments, which enabled purchasers to

mortgage their incomes far ahead of receiving them, and to enjoy the use of goods long before they were paid for. But no such devices could remove the basic maladjustments between the flow
40 of primary and of manufactured goods, nor between the world production of goods which many wanted and the limited power of those who needed them to buy them. The so-called problem of overproduction sprang not from an absence of needs, but from a lack of effective demand. These maladjustments were the basic
45 reason for the economic crash which began in the autumn of 1929, dispelling the growing mood of confidence and prosperity which the previous decade had induced, and toppling over the precarious democratic regimes of central and eastern Europe.

> David Thomson, *Europe Since Napoleon* (London, Pelican, revised edition, 1966), pp 662–3

Questions

a 'The prosperity of the 1920s was real' (line 22). How is this prosperity reflected in extract *a* with regard to 'industrial production'?

b Between 1925 and 1929 the U.S.S.R. (line 6) registered an increase of over 150 per cent in industrial production. To what extent could this reflect increased social welfare in that country?

c With what justification can it be held that increased industrial production, such as illustrated in extract *a*, reflected a belligerent political attitude? Or was it merely the result of a widespread entrepreneurial confidence?

★ d What do statistical documents have to offer to the historian? Why should indices, such as extract *a*, be considered with caution?

e '[B]asic maladjustments' (line 39). Explain in your own words the inherent flaws which marked the otherwise 'growing mood of confidence and prosperity' (line 46) of the 1920s.

f How valid is it to attribute 'the economic crash . . . of 1929' (line 45) to these basic maladjustments?

7 Cultural Disintegration

(a) A contemporary view

The middle classes, in England as elsewhere, under democracy, are morally dependent upon the aristocracy, and the aristocracy are subordinate to the middle class, which is gradually absorbing and destroying them. The lower class still exists; but perhaps it
5 will not exist for long. In the music-hall comedians they find the expression and dignity of their own lives; and this is not found in the most elaborate and expensive revue. In England, at any rate,

the revue expresses almost nothing. With the decay of the music-hall, with the encroachment of the cheap and rapid-breeding cinema, the lower classes will tend to drop into the same state of protoplasm as the bourgeoisie. The working man who went to the music-hall and saw Marie Lloyd and joined in the chorus was himself performing part of the act; he was engaged in that collaboration of the audience with the artist which is necessary in all art and most obviously in dramatic art. He will now go to the cinema, where his mind is lulled by continuous senseless music and continuous action too rapid for the brain to act upon, and will receive, without giving, in that same listless apathy with which the middle and upper classes regard any entertainment of the nature of art. He will also have lost some of his interest in life. Perhaps this will be the only solution. In an interesting essay in the volume of *Essays on the Depopulation of Melanesia*, the psychologist W. H. R. Rivers adduced evidence which has led him to believe that the natives of that unfortunate archipelago are dying out principally for the reason that the 'Civilization' forced upon them has deprived them of all interest in life. They are dying from pure boredom. When every theatre has been replaced by 100 cinemas, when every musical instrument has been replaced by 100 gramophones, when every horse has been replaced by 100 cheap motor-cars, when electrical ingenuity has made it possible for every child to hear its bedtime stories from a loud-speaker, when applied science has done everything possible with the materials on this earth to make life as interesting as possible, it will not be surprising if the population of the entire civilised world rapidly follows the fate of the Melanesians.

'The Decay of the Music-Hall', an excerpt from T. S. Eliot's 'Marie Lloyd' (1923), as reproduced in T. S. Eliot, *Selected Prose*, ed. John Hayward (Harmondsworth, Penguin, 1953), pp 239–40

(b) With the benefit of hindsight

Along with these powerful disintegrating forces which disrupted the international system and the world economy there existed no less powerful forces inside each nation which corroded cultural unity and intellectual integrity, as well as social homogeneity. The nineteen-twenties were marked in Germany by a great social revolution which demolished her middle-class structure and by a moral decline which reduced her greatest cities to centres of vice; in the United States by all the social evils which accompanied the experiment in prohibition; in France by political scandals and a decline in public spirit; in Britain by disputes between capital and labour which culminated in the general strike of 1926; in India by

recurrent riots and by the efforts of Mahatma Gandhi to expel the
British from his country and check industrialization; in European
culture as a whole by exotic experiments in art and literature and
50　neurotic adventures in artistic self-expression. . . .

　　The divorce between the creative artist and his public, which
had shown itself by 1914, now developed into a craze for coteries
and esoteric experiences, of tortured efforts at self-expression
appreciated by only a few and beyond the comprehension of the
55　rest of mankind. In poetry, music, painting, and sculpture the
smooth rhythms and lines of the established forms were regarded
by the new generations of artists as unfitted to express the unrest
and insecurity which, they felt, prevailed in the post-war world.
Free verse, dissonance, surrealism, seemed better adapted to
60　express their vision of truth. Alike in painting and poetry, cubism
led through 'dadaism' to surrealism, proclaiming on the way the
'absurdity of art' and 'the identity of contraries'. Dadaism, initiated
by Tristan Tzara in Switzerland, was both a social and an artistic
rebellion against all conventions. But it expressed in more extreme
65　and anarchical form the same kind of impulse which produced the
music of Stravinsky and Scriabin, the sculpture of Epstein, and the
poetry of the Sitwells. In literature the vogue for D. H. Lawrence
coincided with the growing interest in Freudian psychology and
irrationalism; and James Joyce devoted sixteen years to producing
70　a large work, *Finnegans Wake*, which most readers found quite
incomprehensible.

　　　　David Thomson, *World History from 1914 to 1961* (London,
　　　　Oxford University Press, second edition, 1963), pp 119–21

Questions

a　'The lower class . . . will not exist for long' (lines 4–5).
　　Summarise and explain T. S. Eliot's attitude towards the
　　immediate postwar social and cultural upheaval.
b　Comment briefly on the historical background to (i) 'the
　　experiment in prohibition' (lines 43–4); (ii) the 'political scandals'
　　in France (line 44); (iii) the disputes in Britain 'between capital
　　and labour which culminated in the general strike of 1926' (lines
　　45–6); (iv) 'the efforts of Mahatma Gandhi to expel the British
　　from his country and check industrialization' (lines 47–8).
c　What does Thomson mean by 'exotic experiments in art and
　　literature and neurotic adventures in artistic self-expression'
　　(lines 49–50)?
d　What do the following mean: (i) Free verse (line 59); (ii) dis-
　　sonance (line 59); (iii) surrealism (line 59); (iv) cubism (line 60);
　　(v) 'dadaism' (line 61)? In what sense and with what justification
　　were all these media of 'artistic self-expression' symptomatic
　　of cultural disintegration?

e Who were (i) Stravinsky (line 66); (ii) Scriabin (line 66); (iii) Epstein (line 66); (iv) the Sitwells (line 67); (v) D. H. Lawrence (line 67); (vi) Freud (line 68); (vii) James Joyce (line 69). To what extent were these the product of 'unrest and insecurity which . . . prevailed in the post-war world' (lines 57–8)?

III The Years of the Great Depression 1929–34

Introduction

During the 1920s '[t]he domain of realities,' wrote Wladimir d'Ormesson, one-time editor of the Parisian *Figaro*, 'was rudely abandoned for life in the abnormal. The abnormal reigned so long, however, that one grew accustomed to it and eventually took it for reality. Hence the seductive flow of inflation and the disagreeable ebb of deflation.' The world trade depression and the shattering financial crisis of the end of the decade brought this growing frenzy of false optimism, overconfidence and illusive stability to a grinding halt. The Wall Street Crash of October 1929 would have perhaps constituted an isolated local crisis had not American finance and capital been 'priming the pump' of postwar Europe's 'industrial recovery' throughout the 'roaring Twenties'. Economically, socially and politically the result was devastating for the whole world. World trade was curtailed; banks closed down; industrial progress was curbed; unemployment soared. Rearmament seemed to offer the only reliable and sensible source of employment and a moral compensation for the economic discomfiture. In September 1931 Great Britain went off the gold standard. This was followed by the United States in March 1933. Only Soviet Russia appears to have remained untouched by the economic crisis. Was the Stalinist brand of communism the real solution of world problems? 'In its shattering effect upon European prosperity and stability, the Great Depression was comparable with the Great War itself' (Thomson).

In a sense the Great Depression was a turning point for Italy, Germany and Japan. It mercilessly exposed the inherent flaws in the democratic system of government, while authoritarian Fascist doctrines suggested an attractive alternative to the inept democratic approach to recurrent world problems. Of all the eastern European governments, only Czechoslovakia remained with difficulty loyal to its democratic principles and beliefs. Although the effects of the crisis on France were perhaps not as severe as elsewhere, political instability was rampant, threatening at one moment even the existence of the Republic. The Stavisky affair was a symptom of an ever worsening situation. In Britain the government of Ramsay

MacDonald was given emergency powers to deal with the crisis.

The collapse of German democracy may only partly be attributed to 'the sudden sweep of the Great Depression' although the causal relationship between the two events appears to have been decisive. The crisis in Germany was *sui generis*. Erich Matthias quite rightly calls it permanent and structural. The incurable malaise, he claims, was that the Weimar Republic had 'never succeeded in assimilating its own military and bureaucratic foundations; nor could it ever remove the serious conflicts and tensions between its social and its political structure'. Even without Hitler 'parliamentary democracy would still have been snuffed out' (Carr).

In September 1931, in the midst of financial and economic chaos, Japan began its systematic conquest of Manchuria. This armed conflict constituted the first act in the drama of rising aggression in the 1930s and seriously challenged the raison d'être of the League of Nations, exposing to ridicule the very concept of 'collective security'. In 1933 Japan left the League, whose passivity and severe loss of prestige had spelled out, loud and clear, the organisation's major inherent weaknesses.

[T]he aggressor . . . had defiantly retained his prize, and had departed from Geneva with little more than verbal censure as the price of his deed. In the smaller League states, even in France and Germany as well as Britain and the United States, there was disillusionment and dismay. Whatever the historian may observe at a distance, there is no doubt that in many minds at the time the episode did appear as a turning point; it also provided fresh evidence . . . that the Covenant of the League was a seriously flawed document (Christopher Thorne).

Still in the words of the same historian, the Manchurian crisis 'ensured the failure of the Disarmament Conference', which in May 1934 adjourned indefinitely. By then Germany too had withdrawn both from the Conference and from the League. The student would do well to ask at this stage what had in fact 'paved the way for Hitler's accession to power'. Was it '[o]nly the Great Depression' which, as Taylor claims in *From Sarajevo to Potsdam*, 'put the wind into Hitler's sails'? Or was it more likely the failure of disarmament and, therefore, in an indirect way, the nascent Fascist military power in the Far East that were ultimately responsible? Next it would be Fascist Italy's defiance. Mussolini would soon find the prospect of impunity in foreign conquest too irresistible for his ambition to ignore!

In 1934 Europe found herself at the crossroads, bewildered and uncertain about the morrow, unable to 'find her new balance' (Beneš) but conscious of being 'off on the race' that would end 'in the Olympic games of death' (Knickerbocker). According to H. Stuart Hughes, an American historian, 'by the mid-1930s, the economic and social struggles of the decade were blending imperceptibly into the origins of the Second World War itself'.

1 Plea for the Removal of Restrictions upon European Trade, 1927

We desire, as business men, to draw attention to certain grave and disquieting conditions which, in our judgement, are retarding the return to prosperity.

It is difficult to view without dismay the extent to which tariff
5   barriers, special licences and prohibitions since the war have been allowed to interfere with international trade and to prevent it from flowing in its natural channels. At no period in recent history has freedom from such restrictions been more needed to enable traders to adapt themselves to new and difficult conditions. And at no
10 period have impediments to trading been more perilously multiplied without a true appreciation of the economic consequences involved.

The break-up of great political units in Europe dealt a heavy blow to international trade. Across large areas, in which the inhabitants had been allowed to exchange their products freely, a
15 number of new frontiers were erected and jealously guarded by customs barriers. Old markets disappeared. Racial animosities were permitted to divide communities whose interests were inseparably connected. . . .

To mark and defend these new frontiers in Europe, licences,
20 tariffs and prohibitions were imposed, with results which experience shows already to have been unfortunate for all concerned. One state lost its supplies of cheap food, another its supplies of cheap manufactures. Industries suffered for want of coal, factories for want of raw materials. Behind the customs
25 barriers new local industries were started, with no real economic foundation, which could only be kept alive in the face of competition by raising the barriers higher still. Railway rates, dictated by political considerations, have made transit and freights difficult and costly. Prices have risen, artificial dearness has been
30 created. Production as a whole has been diminished. Credit has contracted and currencies have depreciated. Too many states, in pursuit of false ideals of national interest, have imperilled their own welfare and lost sight of the common interests of the world, by basing their commercial relations on the economic folly which
35 treats all trading as a form of war.

There can be no recovery in Europe till politicians in all territories, old and new, realise that trade is not war but a process of exchange, that in time of peace our neighbours are our customers, and that their prosperity is a condition of our own
40 well-being. If we check their dealings their power to pay their

debts diminishes, and their power to purchase our goods is reduced. Restricted imports involve restricted exports, and no nation can afford to lose its export trade. . . . [W]e cannot view without grave concern a policy which means the impoverishment
45 of Europe.

Happily there are signs that opinion in all countries is awaking at last to the dangers ahead. The League of Nations and the International Chamber of Commerce have been labouring to reduce to a minimum all formalities, prohibitions and restrictions,
50 to remove inequalities of treatment in other matters than tariffs, to facilitate the transport of passengers and goods. In some countries powerful voices are pleading for the suspension of tariffs altogether. . . . And experience is slowly teaching others that the breaking-down of the economic barriers between them may prove
55 the surest remedy for the stagnation which exists.

> Reproduced in Sir George Paish, *The Road to Prosperity* (London, Ernest Benn, 1927), pp 83–6. This appeal was published over the 'signatures of the great bankers, manufacturers and business men of Europe, including Great Britain, as well as of the chief bankers of America'

Questions

a Summarise briefly the arguments given in this extract in favour of freedom of trade.
b What political developments since the war encouraged, according to the 'Plea', 'such restrictions' (line 8) on international trade?
c Identify and comment on (i) 'The break-up of great political units in Europe' (line 12); (ii) 'some countries' (line 51).
d Suggest what the authors of this extract mean by 'false ideals of national interest' (line 32).
★ e 'Happily there are signs that opinion in all countries is awaking . . . to the dangers ahead' (lines 46–7). What other sources would you consult to confirm or disprove this statement?
★ f For what reasons, in your opinion, is knowledge of economic geography a great asset to the student of history?

2 The Great Depression

(a) 1928: 'the last full year of prosperity'

[In 1928] we [the United States] sold about 850 million dollars more goods abroad than we bought. We also had coming to us that year about 200 millions on the war debts, and about 600 millions net return on our foreign investments. How did our
5 foreign consumers and debtors get those 1,650 millions to pay us?

They got 660 millions from the tourists. They got 220 millions from immigrants here who sent money home. . . . Where did they get the rest? They got it out of the 970 millions which we loaned to them that year.

> Walter Lippmann, *Interpretations, 1931–2* (London, Allen & Unwin, 1933), p 46

(b) International repercussions

10   I look at the world to-day and I contrast the conditions now with the conditions at [the] time [of Locarno], and I am forced to acknowledge that for some reason or other, owing to something upon which it is difficult to put one's finger, in these last two years the world is moving backward. Instead of approaching
15   nearer to one another, instead of increasing the measure of goodwill, instead of progressing to a stable peace, it has fallen back into an attitude of suspicion, of fear, of danger, which imperils the peace of the world.

> Sir Austen Chamberlain, the British Foreign Minister, in the *London Times*, 4 February 1932

(c) A near contemporary account

At the end of October [1929] came the sudden end of the Hoover
20   prosperity boom in the United States, when the whole of Wall Street stock-market, not merely a section of it, collapsed. The American public, encouraged by the Republican slogan 'a car in every garage and a chicken in every pot', had been interesting itself in the stock-market and plunging with enthusiastic ignorance.
25   Financiers took advantage of this bullish tendency to drive up the nominal value of stocks to the highest figure possible, in order to unload on the amateur speculators to the very best advantage. They were too successful. When they baled out and allowed the market to find its own level, it crashed disastrously. Hundreds of
30   thousands of Americans lost all their spare cash and then rushed to the banks to be sure at least of their capital; the rush broke the smaller banks by the hundred, and they dragged down many of the larger banks; though no real loss of wealth had taken place, millions of people were ruined and thrown out of employment. . . .
35   [I]t was an international crisis. All over the world, prices were falling; this was leading to an increase in the burden of national debts, and to several cases of national default. World trade was declining, markets shrinking, interest from investments drying up, foreign exchange wobbling. Financial crashes became frequent –
40   the Hatry case was followed by the crash of the British shipowner, Lord Kylsant, and by the failure and suicide of the Swedish match-king, Kreuger. Early in 1931, one of the chief links in the

European banking system snapped – the Austrian Kredit Anstalt.
A loan from the Bank of England and a guarantee from the newly
45 established Bank of International Settlements helped to keep
Austria solvent, but business men lost confidence in Central
Europe. Foreign funds were withdrawn from Germany, which
made the general financial situation more precarious. Italy and
Belgium both had Budget deficits, and nearly all countries were
50 starting serious economy campaigns. President Hoover then put
forward a proposal for a moratorium on the interest and principal
of all inter-governmental debts. Had this been acted upon
immediately it might have eased the situation, but the French
objected on the grounds that they would lose most and the
55 Germans gain most. The financial drain on Germany, in the form
of reparation payments under the Young Plan therefore continued
and German banks began to fail. A conference was called in
London to deal with the German situation. Only the French were
in a position to grant long-term loans, but they wanted political
60 guarantees before they would do so. A deadlock followed. The
effect upon many Germans was to convince them that only a
policy of national self-sufficiency would rid them of the danger of
complete financial and industrial collapse. This feeling the rising
Nazi movement was able to exploit.

> Robert Graves and Alan Hodge, *The Long Week-end: A
> Social History of Great Britain 1918–1939* (London, Penguin,
> 1971), pp 243, 250–1. The book was first published in 1940

Questions

a 'The American public . . . had been . . . plunging with
enthusiastic ignorance' (lines 21–4). To what extent and in
what ways does this judgement explain the illusion of
prosperity revealed by Walter Lippmann in extract *a*?

b 'The Depression had little to do with the preceding war. . . . It
had nothing to do with the surviving provisions of the peace-
treaty' (Taylor). How satisfactory do you find Lippmann's
interpretation of Europe's dependence on American finance
during the first decade or so after the First World War in the
light of Taylor's quotation?

★ c '[T]he whole of Wall Street stock-market . . . collapsed' (lines
20–1). How did such an event in 1929 produce 'an international
crisis' (line 35)?

d What criticism can be made of Sir Austen Chamberlain's brief
account of the 'contrast' (line 10) between the condition of the
world in 1932 and that 'at [the] time [of Locarno]' (line 11)?
Did the 'Great Depression' really imperil 'the peace of the
world'?

e Identify (i) 'the Hatry case' (line 40); (ii) Lord Kylsant (line 41);
(iii) Kreuger (line 42)?

* *f* 'In most countries the Depression led to a turning-away from international affairs' (Taylor). Discuss briefly the effects of the Great Depression on (i) Central Europe; (ii) Italy; (iii) Britain; (iv) France; (v) Germany.

   g Explain and briefly comment on President Hoover's 'proposal for a moratorium' (line 51).

* *h* 'This feeling the rising Nazi movement was able to exploit' (lines 63–4). How did National Socialism in Germany profit from the Great Depression?

3   The World in 1930: Prelude to a Dark Period

All over the world . . . there appeared at first sight to be solid material for satisfaction.

It may, therefore, occasion surprise that this year, 1930, the year when the British Prime Minister had described the risk of war as
5 'practically nil', was the date when the shadow of a possible or probable recurrence of war first began to darken the world. All over Europe, as English travellers in that period reported, the imminence of war was a staple topic of conversation. This was not mere irresponsible rumour. Distinguished financiers, like Dr
10 Somary of Zurich, arrived at a similarly serious diagnosis from the consideration of economic symptoms. In a lecture delivered at Chatham House in December 1930 this authority pointed to the high rate of interest offered in vain by the largest of German banks on guaranteed first mortgage bonds, and drew the conclusion,
15 from this and similar phenomena, that, in the absence of effective steps for the restoration of political confidence, 'the present crisis will be but a prelude to a dark period to which the historian of the future will give the name *Between two Wars*'. A year later the American journalist, Mr Frank Simonds, published his book with
20 the ominous title – *Can Europe keep the Peace?*

What were the reasons for these forebodings? In the first place, some of the items which have been placed on the credit side of the situation must be subjected to qualifications which deprive them of much of their face value. The success of the three-Power naval
25 treaty was equally the failure of the five-Power negotiations, and, by virtue of the 'escalator' clause, the real value of its provisions might depend upon the action taken by the two European Powers, France and Italy, who had failed to reach agreement. Subsequent Franco-Italian discussions on naval limitation, which took place in
30 1930–1, . . . engendered, at various stages, a dangerous amount of heat. Thus, in Florence on 17 May 1930, the question inspired Signor Mussolini to perhaps the most hair-raising of his more truculent utterances:

Words are a very fine thing; but rifles, machine-guns, aeroplanes, and
35   cannon are still finer things. They are finer, Blackshirts, because right
unaccompanied by might is an empty word. . . . Fascist Italy, powerfully
armed, will offer her two simple alternatives: a precious friendship or an
adamantine hostility.

Somewhat similar considerations apply to the conclusion of the
40   draft Disarmament Convention. . . . [T]he final sessions of the
Preparatory Commission showed a dangerous tendency to
rapprochement between Germany, Italy, and the U.S.S.R., and,
though the votes of these three countries were insufficient to
prevent the adoption of the Convention by a majority, a minority
45   consisting of these three Powers was really a much more
formidable obstacle in the path of disarmament than a much larger
opposition, consisting of less powerful States, could have been.
Apart from this, the mere fact that a Commission which had
been appointed five years previously had only achieved a meagre
50   and partial agreement on general principles of limitation by the
end of 1930 was enough to make anyone despair of the prospects
of eliminating armed force from international relations. The
unwillingness of the nations to reduce their armaments was an
indication that no one really placed much trust in the observance
55   of pacts or covenants.

> G. M. Gathorne-Hardy, *A Short History of International
> Affairs 1920–1939* (London, Oxford University Press, fourth
> edition, 1950), pp 259–60. This book was first published in
> 1934

Questions

a   Identify and comment on (i) 'the three-Power naval treaty'
(lines 24–5); (ii) 'the five-Power negotiations' (line 25); (iii) 'the
"escalator" clause' (line 26); (iv) 'a meagre and partial agreement'
(lines 49–50).

b   'What were the reasons for these forebodings?' (line 21).
Summarise the arguments Gathorne-Hardy puts forward in his
attempt to answer this question. How convincing are they?

★ c   '[A] dangerous amount of heat' (lines 30–1). How did 'Franco-
Italian discussions on naval limitation' (line 29) in 1930–31 reflect
(i) France's (ii) Italy's foreign policy?

d   With reference to lines 34–8, do you agree with Denis Mack
Smith's view of Mussolini at this point in time as 'increasingly
belligerent'?

e   How valid historically is it to call the 'tendency to *rapprochement*'
(lines 41–2) between Germany, Italy and the U.S.S.R. in 1930
'dangerous' (line 41)?

4   A Turning Point for Germany

(a) Drift from democracy

[W]hen even the vast capitalist strengths of England and America cannot succeed in keeping their own houses in order, what chance is there for weak and tubercular Germany to accomplish that for herself?

5   There are ... two ways out: Hitler's nationalism, and communism of the Russian brand. Both ideals are represented in Germany by powerful parties backed with considerable funds, able propaganda agents, and trained shock troops and marksmen. Young Germany is choosing between one and the other. Young
10 Germany knows only this one thing: it will not follow the ways of its fathers, it will not pay reparations. The young men had nothing to do with the war, and they will not pay for it. They possess no accumulated wealth or inheritances which could prompt them to cling to the present order, with its moderate safety, rather
15 than fly to revolution and financial crash. They have nothing to lose, and everything to gain, in an overthrow. What they have now is training, and no jobs; a very real Germanic strength, and nothing to apply it to. Overmature for their years, and overnervous and highly-strung in their personalities, they are determined to
20 carry through some reform which might make their lives worth living. . . .
    Thus Germany confesses itself to be in a state of siege. The nation stands alone, and it feels its own foundations slowly weakening under it. It is the sick man of Europe – and its illness is
25 the destiny of our civilization. . . .
    To reduce the German situation to such essentials as these is not to be a professional alarmist; it is merely to admit what everyone realizes today but often likes to gloss over in silence. It is merely to take as basic what the whole world is feeling – skepticism of the
30 power of international accords to cope with the forces of nationalism, French Caesarism, and the eternal hunger for war. It is to take as basic also a greater feeling – the doubt of the capitalist world, the insecurity, the weariness.

> Extract from William Harlan Hale, 'From the Heart of Germany', *The Nation*, 18 November 1931, cxxxiii, pp 355–56

(b) The way to the Right

[I]f the whole German nation today had the same faith in its
35 vocation as these hundred thousands [of SA and SS men of the National Socialist Movement], if the whole nation possessed this idealism, Germany would stand in the eyes of the world otherwise

than she stands now! For our situation in the world in its fatal
effects is but the result of our own underestimate of German
40 strength. Only when we have once more changed this fatal
valuation of ourselves can Germany take advantage of the political
possibilities which, if we look far enough into the future, can
place German life once more upon a natural and secure basis – and
that means either new living-space and the development of a great
45 internal market or protection of German economic life against the
world without and utilization of all the concentrated strength of
Germany. The labour resources of our people, the capacities, we
have them already: no one can deny that we are industrious. . . .

And so in contrast to our own official Government I cannot see
50 any hope for the resurrection of Germany if we regard the foreign
politics of Germany as the primary factor: the primary necessity is
the restoration of a sound national German body-politic armed to
strike. In order to realize this end I founded thirteen years ago the
National Socialist Movement: that Movement I have led during
55 the last twelve years, and I hope that one day it will accomplish
this task and that, as the fairest result of its struggle, it will leave
behind it a German body-politic completely renewed internally,
intolerant of anyone who sins against the nation and its interests,
intolerant against anyone who will not acknowledge its vital
60 interests or who opposes them, intolerant and pitiless against
anyone who shall attempt once more to destroy or disintegrate
this body-politic, and yet ready for friendship and peace with
anyone who has a wish for peace and friendship.

> Extract from Hitler's address to the *Industrieklub* of
> Düsseldorf, 27 January 1932. R. de Roussy de Sales, *Adolf
> Hitler: My New Order* (New York, Reynal & Hitchcock,
> 1941), pp 124–5

Questions

★ a '[W]eak and tubercular Germany' (line 3). What intrinsic
weaknesses in the Weimar Republic became evident by
November 1931?

★ b What do you understand by 'Hitler's nationalism' (line 5)?
What distinguished European communism from the 'communism of the Russian brand' (line 6)?

c How accurate and unbiased is Hale's picture of 'young
Germany'? Is it fair to call it 'the sick man of Europe' (line 24)?
On what grounds does Hale claim that 'its illness is the destiny
of our civilization' (lines 24–5)?

d Explain the historical context of Hale's reference to 'French
Caesarism' (line 31). How did this undermine 'the power of
international accords' (lines 29–30)?

e Explain the meaning of 'SA and SS men of the National

Socialist Movement' (lines 35–6). Suggest what Hitler means by 'faith in its vocation' (lines 34–5) and 'this idealism' (lines 36–7) with reference to the Nazi Movement. Why did Hitler eventually turn against the SA?

f Compare extracts a and b as contemporary explanations of the need for the 'resurrection of Germany'.

★ g 'I founded thirteen years ago the National Socialist Movement' (lines 53–4). What was the attitude of the major political parties in Germany to the rise and consolidation of the National Socialist Movement? What chances did National Socialism have in January 1932 of winning supreme political power in Germany?

5 The Crisis in Germany, 1932

What an abyss between the glowing optimism of those days [i.e., 1929] and the pessimism and despair of today! None of the promises of that period have been realized.

5 The desperate situation which prevails today is evidenced by the number of 25 million unemployed. . . . In Germany this state of things has most strongly shaken the confidence of the masses in the good functioning of the capitalist system. . . .

The world has had to pass through crises in the past. . . . In one essential point, however, the present crisis is different from earlier 10 ones. Formerly we had to deal with crises resulting from a lack of equilibrium between production and consumption, and a period of two to three years was generally sufficient to re-establish equilibrium. But upon the present crisis of international exchange there has been superimposed a second crisis – an unprecedented 1l crisis of credit. This credit crisis has causes peculiar to itself. The most important are the public international debts and political payments, which are contrary to all sound or reasonable economic principles. The crisis of international exchange will not be surmounted unless the credit crisis is also overcome, and the latter 20 cannot be overcome unless the specific cause from which it results is ruthlessly swept aside. This is the first point.

The second point is this. Under the influence of political debts a complete displacement has taken place between debtor and creditor countries in the repartition of gold on the one hand and the 25 exchange of merchandise on the other. Gold has accumulated in the two national economic systems which are creditors under the system of international debts, whereas Germany is today the only debtor country which is almost entirely lacking in gold. In the creditor countries gold has become sterile, and in Germany the 30 absence of gold is causing a growing paralysis of the economic machinery.

On the other hand, the commercial balance of Germany has become favourable during the last two years, under the pressure of its external debt, which is closely linked with the political debts, whereas in former decades it was always unfavourable. In the same period a development in the contrary direction has taken place in the creditor countries. . . .

The German problem is the central problem of the whole of the world's difficulties.

The German situation is characterized by the following:

1. The high level of interest, which crushes agriculture and also industry;

2. The burden of taxation, which is so oppressive . . . that it cannot be increased, but has yet been increased, in order to assure the very existence of the State, by the imposition of fresh taxes within the last few days;

3. The external debt . . . .

4. Unemployment, which is relatively more widespread than in any other country whatever, and which constitutes from 20 to 25 per cent of the population a burden on public funds.

What is particularly fatal is that an ever-growing number of young people have no possibility and no hope of finding employment and earning their livelihood. Despair and the political radicalization of the youthful section of the population are the consequences of this state of things.

> Extract from the speech by von Papen, German Chancellor, to the Lausanne Conference of 16 June–9 July 1932. Reproduced in S. Pollard and C. Holmes (eds), op cit, pp 329–31

Questions

a Explain and briefly comment on the historical significance of the first paragraph.

b Distinguish between (i) the 'crisis of international exchange' (line 13) and the 'crisis of credit' (line 15); (ii) 'external debt' (line 34) and 'political debts' (lines 34–5).

c Identify (i) the 'specific cause' (line 20) which brought about the credit crisis; (ii) the 'two national economic systems' (line 26).

d Summarise von Papen's view on the effect of the Depression on Germany. How far does this conform to your view?

e 'The Depression was Hitler's best ally' (J. A. S. Grenville). Discuss this statement in the light of von Papen's speech and of extracts 4a and 4b.

6   The Manchurian Crisis

(a) Sir Miles Lampson, British Minister in China, June 1933

Japan's great military adventure has, it seems, met with a full
measure of success. She has seized, and to all intents and purposes
secured, a protectorate over Manchuria, rounded off her conquests
by the occupation of Jehol, defied the behests of the League of
5   Nations, and . . . forced the Chinese to admit military defeat and
to accept, at least tacitly and for the time being, the loss of
Manchuria and the *de facto* position created by the Japanese army.
Public Record Office, London, F.O. 371/17064/F6991

(b) Minute by Lawrence Collier, Head, Northern Department (British Foreign Office), 30 October 1934

Japan is the determined enemy of all European interests in China,
including our own, and . . . an understanding with her to
10   safeguard those interests is therefore impossible . . . unless we are
prepared to sacrifice our whole position in the Far East, with
effects which would not be confined to those regions – unless,
indeed, we are prepared to contemplate losing most of our trade
with Asia as a whole, and holding all our Asiatic possessions on
15   sufferance from Japan, we must take every possible step to keep
Japan in check – build up the Singapore base, cultivate good
relations with the Americans, the Dutch, the French and all others
whose interests are threatened with a view to concerted measures
against further Japanese aggression, and . . . see to it, as far as we
20   can, that Russia is kept where she now is, in the Franco-British
orbit, and not allowed to drift into the German-Japanese orbit.
Ibid, F.O. 371/18169/F5943

(c) Churchill's comment

In February, 1933, the League of Nations declared that the State of
Manchukuo could not be recognised. Although no sanctions were
imposed upon Japan, nor any other action taken, Japan, on March
25   27, 1933, withdrew from the League of Nations. Germany and
Japan had been on opposite sides in the war; they now looked
towards each other in a different mood. The moral authority of
the League was shown to be devoid of any physical support at a
time when its activity and strength were most needed.
Winston S. Churchill, *The Second World War*, vol i, *The
Gathering Storm* (London, Cassell, 1948), p 69

(d) A. J. P. Taylor's view

30   [I]n 1933 peace was restored between China and Japan. In later

years the Manchurian affair assumed a mythical importance. It was treated as a milestone on the road to war, the first decisive 'betrayal' of the League, especially by the British government. In reality, the League, under British leadership, had done what the British thought it was designed to do: it had limited a conflict and brought it, however unsatisfactorily, to an end. Moreover, the Manchurian affair, far from weakening the coercive powers of the League, actually brought them into existence. It was thanks to this affair that the League – again on British prompting – set up machinery, hitherto lacking, to organize economic sanctions. This machinery, to everyone's misfortune, made possible the League action over Abyssinia in 1935.

> A. J. P. Taylor, *The Origins of the Second World War* (New York, Fawcett World Library, second edition, 1966), pp 65–66.

Questions

★ *a* How and for what reasons did Japan conquer Manchuria?

★ *b* In what ways did this 'great military adventure' (line 1) defy 'the behests of the League of Nations' (lines 4–5)? What actions did the League take?

★ *c* What were the major 'European interests in China' (line 8)? What was Britain's 'position in the Far East' (line 11)? How were European interests and Britain's position 'threatened' (line 18) by 'Japanese aggression' (line 19)?

★ *d* On what grounds does Lawrence Collier fear that Russia might 'drift into the German-Japanese orbit' (line 21)?

   e Explain 'sanctions' (line 23). Why were no sanctions imposed on Japan? Why did Japan withdraw from the League of Nations?

★ *f* The Far Eastern crisis revealed the inherent weakness of the League of Nations. Explain, and briefly comment on the validity of, Churchill's judgement on 'The moral authority of the League' in lines 27–8.

   g 'On balance the damage caused by the Manchurian episode to the League's prestige was a less serious threat to world peace than the encouragement given to military influences and policies within Japan itself' (Russell Stone). Discuss A. J. P. Taylor's view in extract *d* on the historical importance of the 'Manchurian affair' in the light of Stone's quotation.

7 The Economic Situation in France, June 1934

France appears to have recovered internal stability and to have entered into a period of incipient economic convalescence as the result of the effective grappling, in March and April, 1934, with

the all dominating problem of the disordered public finances and
5 of the ever more menacing budget deficits. The life of the country
had been ravaged by financial disquietude during these very three
or four years when the collapse of world prices and of general
purchasing power, the disablement of several foreign exchanges,
higher tariffs, quotas either for commodities or for foreign
10 payments, and sundry other impediments, were playing havoc
with her home and foreign markets. The restoration of the
abounding prosperity of the years 1922–30 and notably of 1928–30
. . . cannot . . . be anticipated at an early date. Its intensity was
probably due in large measure to the co-operation of certain
15 particular and temporary causes, which may not readily co-exist at
another period in the near future: to depreciation of the French
currency in relation to those of principal customers such as the
United Kingdom, the United States of America, Germany, and
others; to the phenomenal inflation of credit facilities in North and
20 South America and elsewhere; to consequential abnormal demand
for the 'luxury' or semi-luxury goods, of which France is the chief
purveyor, such as silk, laces, fine under and outer clothing,
jewellery, perfumes, wines, spirits; to the efficiency both of the
modern industrial equipment installed throughout French industry
25 as a consequence of war devastation and of the modern French
business spirit and organisation for foreign trade; and, not least, to
the immense yields of the invisible export trade from the inflow of
nearly two million foreign visitors a year.

> Extract from the report *Economic Conditions in France*
> (London, H.M.S.O., 1934) by Sir Robert Cahill.

Questions

a On what grounds, in your opinion, does Sir Robert Cahill
base his impression of economic recovery in France in June
1934 in the first sentence?

★ b 'The life of the country has been ravaged' (lines 5–6). How did
the Depression hit France during the 'three or four years' prior
to June 1934?

c Explain in your own words, and comment briefly on, each of
the factors which, according to Cahill's report, had brought
about 'the abounding prosperity of the years 1922–30 and
notably of 1928–30' (lines 11–12).

8 Europe at the Crossroads, 1934

We are living in a time which is characterized by confusion, by
disorientation of thought and morals, by universal disquiet and
uncertainty. The whole world is simmering, and Europe in
particular cannot find her new balance. Economic self-sufficiency

5   and political nationalism, rising in some countries into paroxysms,
     have strengthened or at least maintained the differences between
     the countries at their old measure. The fight to overthrow the
     international legal order as it now exists is still carried on. The
     economic systems hitherto in vogue have been displaced by new
10   and anti-liberal attempts of a corporative, aetatist, and other
     nature, which in some respects, it is true, answer to the tendencies
     of the day, but which do not solve the economic crisis. Social
     struggles provoke great class shifts, and the levelling process
     continues, strangely enough more intensely where a system of
15   autocratic government obtains than in democracies. The political
     struggle between dictatorship and democracy goes on, and the
     variety of political régimes, especially in Europe, indubitably
     aggravates international tension and difficulties.

> Extract from a speech by Dr Edward Beneš, President and
> Foreign Minister of Czechoslovakia. Reproduced in Robert
> Machray, *The Struggle for the Danube and the Little Entente
> 1929–1938* (London, Allen & Unwin, 1938), pp 160–1

Questions

a   'The whole world is simmering' (line 3). Explain clearly in
    your own words, and comment briefly on the pessimism of,
    Edward Beneš' observation in the opening sentence.
b   Suggest what Beneš had in mind when he referred to (i) 'The
    fight to overthrow the international legal order as it now
    exists' (lines 7–8); (ii) 'The economic systems . . . other nature'
    (lines 8–11); (iii) 'the tendencies of the day' (lines 11–12).
★ c   With reference to the last sentence, discuss briefly the political
    situation in Europe in 1934.
★ d   In what ways does this extract from Beneš' speech reflect the
    general situation in Czechoslovakia?

9   Will Europe go to War?

The armaments race is on. They are off. Germany, France,
Britain, Russia, Japan, Italy, are off on the race that ends in the
Olympic games of death.

     To-day the race is a preliminary. To-morrow it will be the
5   semi-finals. If the contest is not stopped there will be no more
     sense in the question 'Will war come in Europe?' The question
     then will only be '*When* will the war come?' Already the graver
     question has displaced the first in the minds of many observers.

     What are the final results of this investigation that has covered
10   on this Continent every potential battle-field that could be
     foreseen? What is the summary from a visit to a score of Europe's

chief cities and from the opinions gathered in conversation with the men who seek to control the Continent's destiny?

These men spoke for publication. They weighted their words on the side of caution.

President Masaryk, of Czechoslovakia, said: 'There will be no war because there is no money.'

Foreign Minister Benesch, of Czechoslovakia, said: 'Fifty-fifty chance for war in five years.'

His Serene Highness, Regent of Hungary, Admiral Horthy, said: 'There will be no war. It is too great a risk.'

General Camille Walch, Military Governor of Strasbourg, said: 'I am no longer optimistic.'

King Alexander, of Jugoslavia, said: 'No war will start in the Balkans.'

King Boris, of Bulgaria, said: 'War is incredible so long as the generation that experienced the last war is in power.'

Chancellor Dollfuss, of Austria, said the peace of Europe depended on the independence of Austria.

His Majesty, Otto of Habsburg, said the peace of Europe depended on the independence of Austria.

General Joseph Denain, French Minister of Air, said: 'The French Air Fleet is only there for defence. We will reply in kind to any attack. We welcome every new airplane the British build.'

Bogoljub Jeftitch, Foreign Minister of Jugoslavia, asked 'Is peace certain for twelve months?' replied hesitantly, 'I think so.'

Louis Barthou, Foreign Minister of France, said: 'A year ago I wrote that war could not possibly come in 1934. To-day I could no longer express the same opinion.'

Julius Goemboes, Premier of Hungary, asked 'Peace for ten years?', replied, 'I did not say that, but I fervently hope so.'

Mussolini said: 'Peace for ten years.'

Winston Churchill, in the House, said: 'I dread the day. It is not far distant. It is perhaps only a year, or perhaps eighteen months distant.' . . .

Adolf Hitler, to whom the final question of war or peace on this Continent will ultimately be referred, has declared a score of times that he wants peace now and for always. His enemies call Hitler's peace 'the preventive peace'. It is the peace to make the world safe for armaments. Armaments have never left the world safe from war.

> H. R. Knickerbocker, *Will War Come in Europe?* (London, John Lane, [1934]), pp 269–71, 275–6. The above extract is an excerpt from the findings of an investigation undertaken by the International News Service.

Questions

★ *a*   'These men spoke for publication' (line 14). How reliable are such investigations as historical evidence?

★ *b*   What arguments, do you think, would Chancellor Dollfuss and Otto of Habsburg produce in support of their claim that 'the peace of Europe depended on the independence of Austria' (lines 28–9, 30–1)?

   c   To what extent are the reasons given by those who believed there would be no war acceptable to a contemporary political observer?

★ *d*   On what grounds, in your opinion, did politicians such as Beneš (lines 18–19), Walch (lines 22–3), Barthou (lines 37–9) and Churchill (lines 43–5) believe that war was sooner or later inevitable?

   e   'Peace for ten years' (line 42). What amount of credibility would you ascribe to Mussolini's talk of peace in 1934? (See Chapter IV, extract 4*a* and *b*).

   f   With reference to the last paragraph, why should Hitler in 1934 be considered as the sole arbiter of Europe's destiny?

IV Benito Mussolini and Fascist Italy – to 1934

Introduction

On 29 October 1922 Benito Mussolini, the 'man who was [at that moment] leading an armed rebellion against the state' (Mack Smith), was invited by King Vittorio Emanuele to form a government. In less than a year the passage of the so-called Acerbo election law through parliament – by which the strongest party would automatically gain two-thirds of the seats in the Chamber of Deputies – guaranteed Fascism electoral victory and a permanent hold of political power in Italy. With a strong power-seeking ambition, a private army at his disposal 'responsible for countless atrocities throughout Italy' and no political programme, Mussolini found too much of an accommodating disposition in the irresolute and complacent monarchy, beset with anxieties about the political impasse, the Catholic Church, fearful of the horrible prospect of atheistic socialism, and in the 'collective hypnosis' of the 'fragmented and embryonic' parliamentary opposition. 'Fascism's success rested,' says Cassels, 'not on its own strength, but on the ineptitude of its opponents.' In thus allowing Mussolini 'to establish himself in power' the three institutions were accomplices of the Fascist movement. Italy was, ironically, the first western democracy to choose to appease Mussolini and, though not without a brief but fierce fight – the Matteotti crisis provides solid evidence – she was the first to fall prey to that policy.

Apart from its indomitable will to power, Fascism had no clear ideology and was an *ex post facto* doctrine, a political creed which developed gradually to suit rapidly changing circumstances, with Mussolini himself very often falling victim to his own increasingly intensive propaganda. The movement was hostile to liberalism; it denounced parliamentary democracy and disdained Communism. In the *Duce*'s own definition of Fascism, 'the State is an absolute, before which individuals and groups are relative'. To him the State was 'all-embracing', 'totalitarian'; everything else, 'human or spiritual', was valueless outside it. Fascist Italy allowed no political opposition, no press criticism, no free elections. Intense nationalism, exaggerated patriotism and aggressive militarism ranked among the highest values of Fascism. To restore economic stability and to eliminate all friction of social class and party politics, Mussolini constituted Italy into a 'corporate state', subordinating all private interests to the 'nobler' interests of the State. In 1929 Mussolini concluded the still controversial Lateran Agreements with the Catholic Church. Was the Church's 'alliance with fascism . . . a means of maintaining' her 'position' or 'a way of restoring' her 'power in society' (Adrian Lyttelton)?

> The crucifix in the schools [writes Mario G. Rossi], religious teaching, the recognition of the Catholic university, the banning of freemasonry were immediately seen not as final concessions but as the first steps towards the return of the Catholics in society, towards a reconquest that would annul the effects of a sixty years' absence.

Fascism gave Italy what a left-wing historian, masquerading under the Latin name 'Cassius', in 1943 called 'the garish façade of a rejuvenated nation', hoping to revive the 'greatness of Ancient Rome', the 'splendours of the Renaissance' and the 'ideals of the Risorgimento'. It was this same 'Cassius' who first called Fascism 'a fraud' which 'deceived many Italians; but it deceived many more beyond the borders of Italy'. It even deceived the *Duce* himself who was unable in the long run to assess objectively Italy's real strength and that of others.

Mussolini opened, as it were, says Theodor Eschenburg, 'the anti-liberal and anti-democratic struggle in Europe which started in the early 1920s'. It was this and his later aggressive foreign policy which gave the ideology of Fascist totalitarianism a significant place in any study of the origins of the Second World War.

> Fascist Italy [observes Jens Petersen], after an initial phase of internal consolidation, began an expansionist foreign policy from 1925/26 which, impelled powerfully by domestic expectations, demanded political, economic, colonial and territorial expansion and in the long term strove to create an Italian Mediterranean Empire, which was to be reinforced on African soil by the extension of existing colonial possessions.

It was on 5 December 1934 that the question of Walwal arose when Italian and Ethiopian troops clashed on the border between Ethiopia and Italian Somaliland. This minor incident, for which Mussolini had been planning since November 1932, would soon flare up into an international crisis.

1 The Matteotti Crisis

(a) Matteotti at Palazzo Montecitorio, 30 May 1924, 4 p.m.

For the first time Matteotti's high metallic voice became audible: 'Against the validity of this election, we present this pure and simple objection – that the . . . government, nominally with a majority of over four million . . . did *not* obtain these votes, either
5 in fact or freely.'

At once an angry roar . . . filled the Chamber. . . . Motionless, imperturbable, [Premier Benito Mussolini] leaned a face like a death-mask on his hands. . . . Eight weeks earlier, on 6 April, in the first nation-wide election since the March on Rome, the
10 Fascists had benefited richly from Mussolini's new electoral law, designed to assure them a strong working majority. Whichever party polled a plurality – at least twenty-five per cent of the total vote – gained a bonus of two-thirds of the seats in the Chamber. Now . . . the Fascists claimed sixty-four per cent of the popular
15 vote – and 374 seats in the new Chamber. But, with all the oratory at his command, Matteotti was challenging this verdict.

Out of 100 Unitarian Socialist candidates, he charged, sixty had been debarred by Fascist musclemen from canvassing their own districts. One candidate had been gunned down in his own parlour
20 for daring to run for office at all; the first fifteen voters at one polling station, refusing to vote the Fascist ticket, had been thrashed within an inch of their lives. The destruction of Socialist premises had totalled millions of lire. 'No Italian voter was free to decide according to his own will,' Matteotti's voice rang out. 'The
25 Premier had entrusted the custody of the booths to the Fascist militiamen.'

Pandemonium broke loose. . . . Patiently Matteotti told the Chamber: 'I am exposing facts, which should not provoke noise – either the facts are true or you must prove them false.' . . . [F]or
30 every abuse cited he gave chapter and verse, and his charges held the relentless ring of truth. Socialist printing presses had been destroyed, their electoral publicity burned. . . .

Youngsters of twenty had voted in the names of sixty-year-olds. Registration cards had been seized from people afraid to vote
35 and used ten, even twenty, times by Fascist tools voting under different names. He could prove it, Matteotti affirmed – in many instances the handwriting was identical. . . . 'For these reasons, we ask a total cancellation of the election.'

Richard Collier, Duce! The Rise and Fall of Benito Mussolini
(London, Fontana, 1972), pp 71–4

(b) Mussolini's account

The Socialists had been hit on the most sensitive spots; they had

40 been slammed against reality. They were circumscribed in number, amazed by the rush of Italian youth, dismayed by the new directions events were taking. . . . [T]hey were beaten and they felt it. In such a situation, the Socialists wanted to squeeze out the ways of last resort to avoid surrender, at least, in Parliament. . . .

45 One day Matteotti disappeared from Rome. Immediately it was whispered that a political crime had been committed. The Socialists were looking for a martyr who might be of use for their oratory, and at once, before anything definite could possibly be known, they accused Fascism. By my orders we began the most anxious

50 and complete investigations. The Government decided to act with the greatest energy, not only for reasons of justice, but also to stop, from the first moment, the spreading of any kind of calumny. . . . Very soon it was possible to find the guilty. . . . They came from the Fascist group, but they were completely

55 outside our responsible elements.
The sternest proceedings were taken against them without limit or reservation. . . .
All this should have stilled the storm.
On the contrary. This dramatic episode was destined to disturb

60 the austere serenity that I had imposed for myself and for everyone in the general policy of the Country. . . . [T]he opposition threw themselves on the corpse of Matteotti to poison the political life of Italy and cast calumnies on Fascism both in Italy and abroad. . . .
We were going back into the depths of a revolutionary period

65 . . . In December 1924, at the end of that painful three months, some calculated the days of life of our Ministry. A great hope sprang upon the hearts of the politically hungry.

> Benito Mussolini, *My Autobiography*, trans. Richard Washburn Child (London, Hurst & Blackett, 1938), pp 203–8. The book was first published in September 1928

Questions

a Who is Matteotti? What was he doing at Palazzo Montecitorio on 30 May 1924 at 4 p.m.?

★ b '[E]ither the facts are true . . .' (line 29). What value does Matteotti's exposition of the facts regarding 'the validity of this election' (line 2) have as historical evidence?

c Discuss briefly the tone of extract *a* in an attempt to explain its author's attitude to Matteotti.

d 'Fascism had drawn its strength from Socialism's weakness' (Hibbert). Consider briefly the validity and historical significance of the first paragraph of extract *b* in the light of this quotation.

e How and for what reasons did Matteotti disappear from Rome? What consequences did '[t]his dramatic episode' (line 59) have on 'the political life of Italy' (lines 62–3)?

2 Notions about Mussolini and Fascism

Berlin, Monday, 30 October 1922. Mussolini has been appointed Prime Minister by the King of Italy. This may turn out to be a black day for Italy and Europe. . . .

Rome, Tuesday, 15 February 1927. This morning called on Prittwitz at the Embassy. He told me that, although Mussolini's position is entirely secure, he hardly ever now meets a *convinced* Fascist. The fact of a Fascist, corporative state is accepted without argument, but there is great disappointment and disillusionment. The republican trend inside Fascism is gaining ground again. . . .

Rome, Saturday, 26 March 1927. Lunched with Prittwitz alone. I said that I had somehow revised my notions about Mussolini and Fascism. There are elements in the Fascist state, like its corporative structure, which cannot be condemned out of hand. Mussolini moreover does now represent Italy and anyone who wants to be on terms with Italy must come to terms with Mussolini. . . .

Prittwitz agreed with me on both points, adding that people in Germany have been too quick to condemn Fascism out of hand as an entirely reactionary movement. That is not at all the case. On the contrary, it is in many respects an interesting attempt to effect an evolution in the contemporary structure of the state. There is no question of Mussolini being a charlatan; he is genuinely a statesman who, having seriously grappled with the problem of politics and formed his own conclusion, seeks to put it into practice. It is the methods adopted to achieve this objective . . . which are open to criticism. . . .

Italy's complete intellectual stagnation under Fascism, I said, seems to me a very distinct symptom of profound flaws in its intellectual structure. Prittwitz agreed that, as things stand, serious discussion of any political or social problem is utterly out of the question and that this is responsible for the stagnation I mentioned. 'The peace of the graveyard,' I commented. . . . Is Fascism doing anything to improve conditions in Italy? Prittwitz has no doubts whatever about that. Road building, afforestation, and land reclamation are cases in point. Projects are put into execution and do not, as in the past, just remain ideas. Archaeology is also benefiting greatly. Mussolini is an enthusiast about anything that concerns history and the former greatness of Rome. . . . He is not a cultured person or possessed of any deeper traits of refinement, but he is mentally receptive, rendering it pleasant and easy to negotiate with him because he is open to conviction.

The Diaries of a Cosmopolitan: Count Harry Kessler 1918–1937, trans. and ed. Charles Kessler (London, Weidenfeld & Nicolson, 1971), pp 195, 312–13

Questions

a '[A] black day for Italy and Europe' (lines 2–3). What considerations, do you think, influenced Kessler's judgement of Mussolini in October 1922?

b What do you understand by 'a Fascist, corporative state' (line 7)?

c Assess the validity of Prittwitz's definition of Fascism as 'an interesting attempt to effect an evolution in the contemporary structure of the state' (lines 19–20).

d What criticism would you make of Mussolini's 'methods . . . to achieve this objective' (line 24)?

e 'The peace of the graveyard' (line 31). Consider the historical validity of this view of Italy under Fascism down to 1927.

f What contribution does this extract make to your notion of Mussolini and Fascism?

3   The Lateran Agreements, 11 February 1929

(a) The Treaty of the Lateran

Article 1. Italy recognises and reaffirms the principle . . . according to which the Roman Catholic Apostolic religion is the sole religion of the State.

Art. 2. Italy recognizes the sovereignty of the Holy See in
5   international domain . . . .

Art. 3. Italy recognizes the full ownership and the exclusive and absolute dominion . . . of the Holy See over the Vatican . . . .

Art. 8. Considering the person of the Supreme Pontiff as sacred and inviolable, Italy declares any attempt against the same, and
10   any incitement to commit such an attempt, to be punishable with the same penalties as are prescribed in the case of an attempt . . . against the person of the King . . . .

Art. 11. The central bodies of the Catholic Church shall be exempt from any interference on the part of the Italian State . . . .

(b) Concordat between the Holy See and Italy

15   *Art. 1.* Italy shall assure to the Catholic Church the free exercise of spiritual power and the free and public exercise of worship, as well as of its jurisdiction in ecclesiastical matters . . . .

Art. 2. The Holy See shall communicate and correspond freely with the bishops, the clergy and the whole Catholic world without
20   any interference on the part of the Italian Government . . . .

Art. 19. The selection of archbishops and bishops shall appertain to the Holy See.

Art. 34. Desiring to restore to the institution of marriage, which is

the basis of the family, a dignity in conformity with the Catholic
25 traditions of the people, the Italian State recognizes the civil effects
of the sacrament of marriage as governed by canon law . . . .

Both extracts from *British and Foreign State Papers*, vol cxxx
(1929), Part 1, pp 791–814

(c) An assessment

Mussolini thus disarmed, without firing a shot, one of the most
potentially dangerous opponents to the regime, and Fascism was
assured of the adhesion of the Catholic masses under the leadership
30 of a clergy which was in the majority substantially devoted to it. It
was not by accident that the plebiscitary elections, which were
held immediately after the Conciliation to elect a Chamber based
on the new system of a single list of candidates chosen by the
Party, were a clamorous success for Mussolini and Fascism, a
35 success which could not be explained away exclusively in terms of
the absolute lack of political freedom. A considerable number of
the affirmative votes were genuine, and the contribution of the
new Catholic votes was certainly not among the least decisive.

However, in the long run, the agreement with the Church also
40 constituted an element of weakness for the regime. Once again,
Fascism gave up even attempting to ensure the monopoly of
consciences for itself and formally accepted to live alongside an
institution of profoundly different ideological convictions and
which because it was so firmly rooted in the very tissues of Italian
45 life, could not but constitute a serious limitation to its totalitarian
aspirations.

Extract from Alberto Aquarone, 'Mussolini's Italy', in
History of the 20th Century (BPC Publishing Ltd, 1968),
pp 1086–7

Questions

a Distinguish between a 'treaty' and a 'concordat'.
b '[O]ne of the most potentially dangerous opponents to the
regime' (lines 27–8). Explain briefly the major ideological
differences between Fascism and Catholicism.
c Comment briefly on the relations between the Holy See and
Fascist Italy until 1929.
d Consider the circumstances which induced the Catholic Church
to conclude the Lateran Agreements with Fascist Italy. What
did the Church gain by these Agreements?
e How did Mussolini profit from the Lateran Agreements?
★ f Assess the validity of Aquarone's claim that 'in the long run,
the agreement with the Church . . . constituted an element of
weakness for the regime' (lines 39–40).

4 Early Foreign Policy

(a) Mussolini's view

The foreign policy of Italy, directed by me, has been simple, understandable, and rests on these main points:

First, mine is a policy of peace. It is founded not upon words, gestures, and mere paper transactions, but comes from an elevated
5 national prestige and from a whole network of agreements and treaties which cement harmony between peoples.

Secondly, I have not made any specific alliances with the Great Powers. Instead, I have negotiated a series of treaties which show a clear and decisive will to assure to Italy a prosperity in its
10 relations with all nations, especially with those of great historical importance such as England.

Nor have I failed to work out a whole series of treaties with minor Powers, so that Italian influence could have its part in general progress. Albania is one case. Hungary and Turkey are
15 others. To assure harmony on the Mediterranean I have established accords with Spain; to make possible a greater development of our industries and of our foreign trade, I resumed independent commercial relations with Russia.

Stupid indeed are those who fail to see that I have taken a
20 serene, respectful attitude, but not a humble one. The League of Nations and some of the diplomacy inspired by the Locarno Treaty are witnesses of that. I made reservations, after meditated discussions, and because of my grounded beliefs as to the pacts of disarmament, I noticed some absurdities in them.

Benito Mussolini, *My Autobiography*, pp 237–8

(b) The view of Mussolini's biographer

25 By 1925 [Mussolini] had formulated the basic principles of fascist policy towards the outside world. The aim was 'to found an empire', to win 'glory and power', 'to create in the laboratory a new generation of warriors ready at any moment to lay down their lives'. The essence of fascism was said to be a 'military style'.
30 'It is a crime not to be strong', and all Italians should consider themselves mobilized even in peacetime, while he himself intended to raise their military efficiency 'to the very limit of what is possible'. 'Peacemongering' was folly. He was going to build an air force that would 'dominate the skies', and Italians must learn to
35 feel themselves to be 'in a permanent state of war' as they moved towards making this 'the century of Italian power'. One possibility in his mind was that the whole of Europe might become a powerful fascist bloc. Fascism was a creed that was bound to spread throughout the world, and he believed that even Britain
40 and France were abandoning liberal ideals as they were forced to

accept that parliamentary government no longer worked. Any
contradictory evidence from foreign countries was rarely brought
to his attention or mentioned in the Italian press; on the contrary,
there was the daily and monotonous reiteration that fascism was
45   everywhere either feared or admired.
Denis Mack Smith, *Mussolini*, p 115

Questions

   a Distinguish between 'agreements', 'treaties' and 'alliances'.
★ *b* Comment briefly on Fascist Italy's political relations with
     Great Britain down to 1928. How did such relations benefit
     Mussolini's designs?
★ *c* How did Fascist Italy profit from its 'treaties' with (i) Albania;
     (ii) Hungary; (iii) Turkey; and (iv) Spain? In what ways did
     Russia contribute towards Fascist Italy's industrial and
     commercial development?
   d Is there any evidence, other than Mussolini's own confession
     in extract *a*, to support the view that his attitude and approach
     to foreign policy was 'serene, respectful . . . but not . . .
     humble' (line 20)?
★ *e* 'Fascism . . . was bound to spread throughout the world'
     (lines 38–9). What was the general attitude of public opinion in
     Britain and France to Fascism?
   f In the light of extract *b*, what criticism would you make of
     Mussolini's account of his early foreign policy as given in
     extract *a*?

5 Mussolini on Fascism

(a) Humanity is . . . an abstraction of time and space; men are still
not brothers, do not want to be, and evidently can not be. Peace is
hence absurd or rather it is a pause in war. There is something
which binds man to his destiny of struggling. The motives of the
5   struggle may change indefinitely; they may be economic, religious,
political, sentimental, but the legend of Cain and Abel seems to be
the unescapable reality while 'brotherhood' is a fable. . . . The
Christian and Socialist 'men be brothers' is a mask for the eternal
and immutable *homo homini lupus* . . . and man will continue to be
10 a wolf among wolves for a bit of land, for a trickle of water, for a
crumb of bread, for a woman's kiss, for a necessity – or a caprice.
Quoted in H. W. Schneider, *Making the Fascist State* (New
York, Oxford University Press, 1928), pp 274, 275

(b) Above all Fascism . . . believes neither in the possibility nor
the utility of perpetual peace. It thus repudiates the doctrine of

Pacifism – born of a renunciation of the struggle and an act of
15 cowardice in the face of sacrifice. War alone brings up to its
highest tension all human energy and puts the stamp of nobility
upon the people who have the courage to meet it. All other trials
are substitutes, which never really put men into the position
where they have to make the great decision – the alternative of life
20 and death. Thus a doctrine which is founded upon the harmful
postulate of peace is hostile to Fascism. . . . And thus hostile to
the spirit of Fascism . . . are all international leagues and societies,
and societies which, as history will show, can be scattered to the
winds when once strong national feeling is aroused by any
25 motive – sentimental, ideal or practical. . . . Thus the Fascist
accepts life and loves it, knowing nothing of and despising suicide;
he rather conceives life as duty, and struggle and conquest.
> Benito Mussolini, *Fascism*, translated in *International
> Conciliation*, 1935, pp 7, 8

Questions

a What, according to Mussolini, were the principles underlying
Fascism?

★ b Explain the main differences between (i) Christian ideology
and Socialism; (ii) Socialism and Fascism.

★ c Fascism 'repudiates the doctrine of Pacifism (lines 13–14). In
the light of this statement, discuss briefly Fascist Italy's position
in 'international leagues and societies' (line 22) until 1935.

d What impression of Mussolini do you get from these extracts?

★ e To what extent and in what ways was Mussolini a real threat
to international peace and stability by 1935?

6 Fascism – Two Views

(a) An ideology

An unwillingness to familiarize ourselves with the published work
of the young Mussolini himself has left us with a shallow and
inaccurate assessment of the ideological foundations of the first
mass-mobilizing, modernizing movement of our century. . . .

5 Whatever it subsequently became, the first Fascism was an
ideology capable of tapping the broad-based sentiments of outrage
born of what Mirko Ardemagni was later to call Italy's 'ancient
humiliations,' the slavery, submissiveness, and impotence Italy
had endured for centuries. Fascism was, for millions of Italians, a
10 promise of relief from that sense of vulnerability suffered by all
peoples locked in underdevelopment. It heralded increased control
over processes that had hitherto brought only distress to the vast
majority of the population. It augured redemptive change, a

refashioning of the fragile unity with which Italy had entered the
15 new century. . . . Fascism provided a sense of continuity by
identifying itself with the historical traditions of the nation, and
yet it presented itself as a thoroughly modern and revolutionary
innovation. With its promise of modernisation, an increase in
international status, and the expansion of productive capacity
20 Fascism was able to collect around itself every vital segment of the
community. The sure conviction of their own competence allowed
the first Fascists to allay the pervasive sense of inferiority and
inadequacy that still afflicted so many newly urbanized and recently
displaced population elements. Its programme of expansion was
25 sufficiently attractive to the established industrial elite, the
white-collar bourgeoisie, the small entrepreneurial classes, the
professionals, the dislocated intelligentsia, large segments of the
organized working class, and the large and small landholding
agrarians, to rapidly assure its success. Having won the support of
30 the young, the recently demobilized, the active military, and the
constabulary, having neutralized the Catholic populists and the
forces that supported parliamentarianism, and having defeated
organized socialism, there remained no force on the peninsula
capable of resisting Mussolini's Fascism.

> A. James Gregor, *Young Mussolini and the Intellectual Origins
> of Fascism* (Berkeley, University of California, 1979),
> pp 251–2

(b) A fraud

35 Fascism never possessed the ruthless drive, let alone the material
strength, of National Socialism. Morally it was just as corrupting –
or perhaps more so from its very dishonesty. Everything about
Fascism was a fraud. The social peril from which it saved Italy
was a fraud; the revolution by which it seized power was a fraud;
40 the ability and policy of Mussolini were fraudulent. Fascist rule
was corrupt, incompetent, empty; Mussolini himself a vain,
blundering boaster without either ideas or aims. Fascist Italy lived
in a state of illegality; and Fascist foreign policy repudiated from
the outset the principles of Geneva. Yet Ramsay MacDonald
45 wrote cordial letters to Mussolini – at the very moment of
Matteotti's murder; Austen Chamberlain and Mussolini exchanged
photographs; Winston Churchill extolled Mussolini as the saviour
of his country and a great European statesman. How could anyone
believe in the sincerity of Western leaders when they flattered
50 Mussolini in this way and accepted him as one of themselves? . . .
The presence of Fascist Italy at Geneva, the actual presence of
Mussolini at Locarno, were the extreme symbols of unreality in
the democratic Europe of the League of Nations.

> A. J. P. Taylor, op cit, pp 59–60

Questions

a   How far do you agree with the first sentence of extract *a*? How useful and reliable is 'the published work of the young Mussolini' (lines 1–2) as historical evidence to the student of 'the first Fascism' (line 5)?

★ b   Distinguish between 'the first Fascism' and the later Fascism.

c   What positive features of Fascism can you discern from extract *a*?

★ d   '[T]here remained no force on the peninsula capable of resisting Mussolini's Fascism' (lines 33–4). What were the problems facing 'the first Fascism'? How were these eventually overcome?

e   Consider carefully the first sentence of extract *b* in an attempt to explain (i) the similarities; (ii) the main differences between Fascism and National Socialism.

f   'Everything about Fascism was a fraud' (lines 37–8). Identify and, in the light of this statement, comment on (i) 'The social peril from which it saved Italy' (line 38); (ii) 'the revolution by which it seized power' (line 39).

g   What considerations, do you think, influenced A. J. P. Taylor's assessment of 'Fascist rule' in line 40 and of 'Mussolini himself' in lines 40–2? How tenable are these judgements historically?

★ h   '[T]he extreme symbols of unreality' (line 52). Would you agree that (i) Britain's relations with Fascist Italy; (ii) 'The presence of Fascist Italy at Geneva' (line 51); and (iii) 'the actual presence of Mussolini at Locarno' (lines 51–2) constituted a betrayal of the spirit and principles of Geneva?

7   Preparation for War

It is, therefore, necessary to be prepared for war not to-morrow but to-day. We are becoming – and shall become so increasingly because this is our desire – a military nation. A militaristic nation, I will add, since we are not afraid of words. To complete the
5   picture, war-like – that is to say, endowed ever to a higher degree with the virtues of obedience, sacrifice, and dedication to country. This means that the whole life of the nation, political, economic, and spiritual, must be systematically directed towards our military requirements. War has been described as the Court of Appeal but
10   pursue the course dictated by their strength and by their historical dynamic nature, it falls that, in spite of all conferences, all protocols, and all the more or less highest and good intentions, the hard fact of war may be anticipated to accompany the human kind in the centuries to come just as it stands on record at the
15   dawn of human history.

Extract from Mussolini's speech to the General Staff, *The Times*, 28 August 1934, reproduced in *Documents on*

International Affairs, 1928–39 (London, Royal Institute of International Affairs, 1929–54), *Documents 1934*, p 326

Questions

a What do you consider to have been Italy's 'military requirements' (lines 8–9) by August 1934?
b How could 'the whole life' (line 7) of Fascist Italy be 'systematically directed' (line 9) towards these 'requirements' politically, economically and spiritually?
c What impression of the state of Fascist Italy in 1934 do you get from this extract? How far, and for what reasons, could Mussolini be taken as a serious threat to international peace at this particular point in time?

8 The Fascists' *Ten Commandments*

(a) The 1934 version

1. Know that the Fascist, and in particular the soldier, must not believe in perpetual peace.
2. Days of imprisonment are always deserved.
3. The nation serves even as a sentinel over a can of petrol.
5   4. A companion must be a brother, first, because he lives with you, and secondly because he thinks like you.
5. The rifle and cartridge belt, and the rest, are confided to you not to rust in leisure, but to be preserved in war.
6. Do not say 'The Government will pay . . .' because it is *you*
10   who pay; and the Government is that which you willed to have, and for which you put on a uniform.
7. Discipline is the soul of armies; without it there are no soldiers, only confusion and defeat.
8. Mussolini is always right.
15   9. For a volunteer there are no extenuating circumstances when he is disobedient.
10. One thing must be dear to you above all: the life of the Duce.

(b) The 1938 version

1. Remember that those who fell for the revolution and for the empire march at the head of your columns.
20   2. Your comrade is your brother. He lives with you, thinks with you, and is at your side in the battle.
3. Service to Italy can be rendered at all times, in all places, and by every means. It can be paid with toil and also with blood.
4. The enemy of Fascism is your enemy. Give him no quarter.

25 5. Discipline is the sunshine of armies. It prepares and illuminates
the victory.
6. He who advances to the attack with decision has victory
already in his grasp.
7. Conscious and complete obedience is the virtue of the
30 Legionary.
8. There do not exist things important and things unimportant.
There is only duty.
9. The Fascist revolution has depended in the past and still
depends on the bayonets of its Legionaries.
35 10. Mussolini is always right.

> Reproduced in *Sources of Western Civilization*, eds Daniel D.
> McGarry and Clarence L. Hohl, Jr (Boston, Houghton
> Mifflin Co., 1963), pp 398–9

Questions

a Compare and contrast the two versions of the Fascists' *Ten
Commandments*.
b From a close reading of both extracts, arrive at a definition of
Fascism.
c What do the two extracts reflect on the nature and methods of
Fascism?

V   The Rise to Power of Adolf Hitler

Introduction

On 30 January 1933, barely two months after National Socialism had suffered a startling reversal in popular support, President Hindenburg appointed Adolf Hitler, the 'rabid rabble-rousing politician' (Grenville) Chancellor of the languishing Weimar Republic. According to Elizabeth Wiskemann, the impact of his appointment on the psychology of all German-speaking peoples, in and outside Germany, must have been enormous. It stimulated their many 'aspirations and grievances'. Hitler's fiasco at the Beer Hall Putsch had ironically 'glamorised' his ignominious past and turned him into 'a national figure . . . a patriot and a hero' (Shirer). His political dexterity had converted his trial for treason at Munich into 'a political triumph' (Bullock), perhaps one of his greatest successes. His subsequent months at the Bavarian fortress of Landsberg am Lech gave him the opportunity of describing in *Mein Kampf* the aims and development of National Socialism.

The abortive *Putsch* was a lesson in political maturity. There would be no second failure. 'Total power' would be gained behind a legal facade and 'national revolution' realised through the ballot-box. The Weimar Constitution would be overthrown not by violence but through its own entrenched provisions. He would thereby maintain the semblance of legality. Within less than two months of his appointment, the 'Enabling Act' was passed through the Reichstag with its necessary two-thirds majority, conferring on Hitler exclusive legislative powers for four years. This gave him ample time 'to establish his dictatorship by consent of Parliament'. Hindenburg died conveniently on 2 August 1934 and Hitler assumed full presidential powers. The man who had become Chancellor 'almost by accident' (Wiskemann), the hysterical racialist, pathologically obsessed with *Lebensraum* and hatred of democracy and Marxism, was now the absolute dictator of Germany.

How can Hitler's meteoric rise to power be explained? Like any other man great or small, Hitler cannot be abstracted from his world if one wishes to attain an objective perspective. In the first place, the political and economic weaknesses of the Weimar

Republic were much stronger contributory factors than either his increasingly 'restive' popular support (the Nazis had lost two million votes in November 1932), or any national revolutionary movement. His political rivals, who were generally divided and ineffective, grossly underestimated his satanic, monstrous qualities. The Nationalist Right were perhaps most to blame for their 'willingness . . . to accept him as a partner in government' (Bullock). Genuine fear of Communism encouraged powerful German industrial magnates and Junker landowners to lend the Nazi Party, which they considered useful to their interests, 'large-scale financial support'. Other favourable circumstances included the Great Depression, which by the end of 1931 had already created mass unemployment in Germany, the League of Nations' incapacity at containing the daring Japanese military confrontation in the Far East, and the failure of the Disarmament Conference. The student should consider carefully each of these 'circumstances' to be able to assess their individual and collective impact. Which of these factors, for example, made Hitler's rise to power *possible*? Which of them made his triumph *inevitable*? Hitler, claims E. Deuerlein, 'arose more out of the possibilities of the situation than out of the capabilities in himself . . . a historical situation did not exactly produce him but it made him possible.'

Hitler's success [writes Lothar Kettenacker] was due, to a large extent, to the fact that he was constantly misjudged by his enemies: by the left he was seen as a mere tool in the hands of capitalism, by the conservatives as an inexperienced, incompetent demagogue with a mass following. By foreign statesmen in the 1930s he was seen as a Machiavellian revisionist who tried to annul the results of the Versailles treaty.

There is still ample room for wide differences of opinion about the real aims of Germany's foreign policy after 1933. Was Hitler's foreign policy, for example, the systematic realisation of a long-range programme, the gradual achievement of a grandiose political design, as the so-called Hossbach Protocol suggests? To what extent, if any, did Hitler's approach depart from the German tradition? 'In this sphere alone,' claims A. J. P. Taylor, 'he changed nothing. His foreign policy was that of his predecessors'. John Hiden rejects the 'continuity' theory. 'It is impossible to overlook the racist and revolutionary ideology which underpinned Hitlerian expansion.' Hans-Adolf Jacobsen defines German foreign policy between 1933 and the end of the war as 'a revolutionary break'. On at least four aims most historians seem to be in agreement: the restoration of 'the armed strength of Germany'; the annulment of 'those parts of the Versailles Settlement which he disliked'; Pan-Germanism or the extension of 'the Reich to include all Germans'; and the frantic search for *Lebensraum* in eastern and southeastern Europe.

Hitler's views on foreign affairs, explains Erich Matthias, were basically those 'which he had developed long before 1933. He never abandoned ambitions to realise his old aims'. Matthias emphasises the 'decisive importance' of this observation in view of later developments. 'This means that Germany started on her road into the catastrophe of the Second World War not in 1938 or 1939 but in 1933' when Adolf Hitler became Chancellor.

1   The Beer-Hall Putsch

(a) 'A revolution by sheer bluff' – the night 8–9 November 1923

The National Revolution, (Hitler shouted), has begun. This hall is occupied by six hundred heavily armed men. No one may leave the hall. The Bavarian and Reich Governments have been removed and a provisional National Government formed. The Army and
5   police barracks have been occupied, troops and police are marching on the city under the swastika banner. . . .

The Bavarian Ministry is removed. I propose that a Bavarian government shall be formed consisting of a Regent and a Prime Minister invested with dictatorial powers. I propose Herr von
10   Kahr as Regent and Herr Pohner as Prime Minister. The government of the November Criminals and the Reich President are declared to be removed. A new National Government will be nominated this very day, here in Munich. A German National Army will be formed immediately. . . . I propose that, until
15   accounts have been finally settled with the November criminals, the direction of policy in the National Government be taken over by me. Ludendorff will take over the leadership of the German National Army. Lossow will be German Reichswehr Minister, Seisser Reich Police Minister. The task of the provisional German
20   National Government is to organize the march on that sinful Babel, Berlin, and save the German people. . . . Tomorrow will see either a National Government in Germany or us dead.

> Reproduced in Alan Bullock, *Hitler: A Study in Tyranny*
> (Harmondsworth, Penguin, revised edition, 1962), pp 106–
> 108. The above text 'is based,' says Bullock, 'on the
> subsequent court proceedings in Munich: *Der Hitler-Prozess*'

(b) 'Born to be a dictator'

How petty are the thoughts of small men. Believe me, I do not regard the acquisition of a Minister's portfolio as a thing worth
25   striving for. I do not hold it worthy of a great man to endeavour to go down in history just by becoming a Minister. One might be

in danger of being buried beside other Ministers. I aimed from the
first at something a thousand times higher than a Minister. I
wanted to become the destroyer of Marxism. I am going to
30   achieve this task, and if I do, the title of Minister will be an
absurdity as far as I am concerned. When I stood for the first time
at the grave of Richard Wagner my heart overflowed with pride in
a man who had forbidden any such inscription as: Here lies Privy
Councillor, Music-Director, His Excellency Baron Richard von
35   Wagner. I was proud that this man and so many others in German
history were content to give their names to history without titles.
It was not from modesty that I wanted to be a drummer in those
days. That was the highest aspiration: the rest is nothing.

     The man who is born to be a dictator is not compelled; he wills
40   it. He is not driven forward, but drives himself. There is nothing
immodest about this. Is it immodest for a worker to drive himself
towards heavy labour? Is it presumptuous of a man with the high
forehead of a thinker to ponder through the nights till he gives the
world an invention? The man who feels called upon to govern a
45   people has no right to say: If you want me or summon me, I will
cooperate. No, it is his duty to step forward.

         Hitler's closing speech during the court proceedings,
         Munich 1924, reproduced in Alan Bullock, op cit, p 117

Questions

a   Who were the 'November Criminals' (line 11) and what
    'accounts' (line 15) did Hitler hope to settle with them?

b   Explain and comment briefly on 'that sinful Babel' in lines 20–1.

c   Illustrate the political circumstances which encouraged the
    National Socialists' attempt to overthrow 'the Bavarian and
    Reich Governments' in November 1923. Account briefly for
    its failure.

★ d   'By the time [his trial] had ended twenty-four days later Hitler
    had transformed defeat into triumph' (Shirer). Discuss briefly.

e   'That was the highest aspiration' (line 38). Why, in your opinion,
    does Hitler consider his role of 'a drummer' (line 37) of utmost
    importance?

★ f   'I wanted to become the destroyer of Marxism' (lines 28–9).
    How real was the threat of Communism in Germany in the early
    1920s?

g   What impressions of Hitler's (i) character; (ii) qualities; and
    (iii) ideas at this stage in his career do you derive from these
    extracts?

h   Hitler's stay in Landsberg prison 'had done him a world of
    good' (Ludecke). In the light of this quotation, how important
    do you consider the Beer-Hall Putsch to have been in Hitler's
    rise to power?

2 The Appeal of National Socialism

(a) On November 9th, 1923, four and a half years after its foundation, the German National Socialist Labour Party was dissolved and
forbidden throughout the whole of the Reich. Today, in November
1926, it is again established throughout the Reich, enjoying full
5   liberty, stronger and internally more compact than ever before.

All persecutions of the Movement and the individuals at its
head, all the imputations and calumnies, have not been able to
prevail against it. Thanks to the justice of its ideas, the integrity of
its intentions and the spirit of self-denial that animates its members,
10 it has overcome all oppression and increased its strength through
the ordeal. If, in our contemporary world of parliamentary
corruption, our Movement remains always conscious of the
profound nature of its struggle and feels that it personifies the
values of individual personality and race, and orders its action
15 accordingly – then it may count with mathematical certainty on
achieving victory some day in the future. And Germany must
necessarily win the position which belongs to it on this Earth if it
is led and organized according to these principles.

A State which, in an epoch of racial adulteration, devotes itself
20 to the duty of preserving the best elements of its racial stock must
one day become the ruler of the Earth.

> Adolf Hitler, *Mein Kampf*, trans. James Murphy (London,
> Hurst and Blackett, 1939), p 560

(b) [Hitler] made his success possible by the happy fluke or
unconscious inspiration . . . of organising [the members of the
lower middle class], not on a class basis against the workers and
25 the aristocrats, but on a broadly national basis which could be
indefinitely enlarged to include all elements within the community
. . . He saw the *petite bourgeoisie* – the salaried classes, the small
shopkeepers, the farmers and the peasants – were crying for
organisation just as much as the factory proletariat were. He
30 offered them *Folkic* as opposed to trade union organization, and
later enwidened his organization to take in all sections – whether
proletarian or even aristocratic – who were ready to place patriotic
over class interests. This benevolent inclusiveness – like the
amorphous pantheism of some Asiatic religion – gained him more
35 and more adherents, so that at last his rally of the *Kleinbürgertum*
could be reinterpreted as the rise of the nation. . . . He solved the
neurosis of a single class by invoking the idea of renascent
Nationalism and discovered that the panacea he had hit upon
could be indefinitely expanded. From being the lord of the
40 *Kleinbürgertum* he became the Führer of the nation as a whole.

> S. H. Roberts, *The House that Hitler Built* (New York,
> Harper & Brothers, 1938), p 44

Questions

★ *a* '[I]t is again established throughout the Reich' (line 4). What factors assisted the re-emergence of National Socialism in the Weimar Republic in the years 1923–26?

b What do you think Hitler intended to suggest by (i) 'our contemporary world of parliamentary corruption' (lines 11–12; (ii) 'an epoch of racial adulteration' (line 19)?

c Explain (i) *Folkic* (line 30); (ii) *Kleinbürgertum* (lines 35, 40).

d What do extracts *a* and *b* add to your knowledge of Hitler's qualities as a political leader?

e Assess the value of each of the two extracts to a historian examining the rise to power of National Socialism.

3   Hitler Assails Democracy

Democracy, as practised in Western Europe to-day, is the forerunner of Marxism. In fact the latter would not be conceivable without the former. Democracy is the breeding ground in which the bacilli of the Marxist world pest can grow and spread. By the
5   introduction of parliamentarianism democracy produced an abortion of filth and fire, the creative fire of which, however, seems to have died out. . . .

Is it at all possible actually to call to account the leaders of a parliamentary government for any kind of action which originated
10   in the wishes of the whole multitude of deputies and was carried out under their orders or sanction? Instead of developing constructive ideas and plans, does the business of a statesman consist in the art of making a whole pack of blockheads understand his projects? Is it his business to entreat and coax them so that they
15   will grant him their generous consent?

Is it an indispensible quality in a statesman that he should possess a gift of persuasion commensurate with the statesman's ability to conceive great political measures and carry them through into practice?
20   Does it really prove that a statesman is incompetent if he should fail to win over a majority of votes to support his policy in an assembly which has been called together as the chance result of an electoral system that is not always honestly administered? . . .

In this world is not the creative act of the genius always a
25   protest against the inertia of the mass? . . .

Must not our parliamentary principle of government by numerical majority necessarily lead to the destruction of the principle of leadership?

Does anybody honestly believe that human progress originates
30   in the composite brain of the majority and not in the brain of the individual personality? . . .

The parliamentary principle of vesting legislative power in the decision of the majority rejects the authority of the individual and puts a numerical quota of anonymous heads in its place. . . .

35 One truth which must always be borne in mind is that the majority can never replace the man. The majority represents not only ignorance but also cowardice. And just as a hundred blockheads do not equal one man of wisdom, so a hundred poltroons are incapable of any political line of action that requires
40 moral strength and fortitude.

Adolf Hitler, *Mein Kampf*, pp 78, 79, 80, 81

Questions

★ *a* Explain and comment on the historical validity of Hitler's claim in the first sentence.

b What, according to this extract, are Hitler's views on the ultimate 'business' (line 14) of a statesman?

c How does this extract convey Hitler's 'contempt for the ideals of democracy' and his 'instinct of tyranny'?

4 The Rising of a Nation

(a) Hitler appointed Chancellor, 30 January 1933

It seems like a dream. The Chancellory is ours. The Leader is already working [there]. We stand in the window upstairs, watching hundreds and thousands of people march past the aged President of the Reich and the young Chancellor in the flaming
5 torchlight, shouting their joy and gratitude.

At noon we are all at the Kaiserhof, waiting. The Leader is with the President of the Reich. The inward excitement almost takes our breath away. In the street the crowd stands silently waiting between the Kaiserhof and the Chancellory. What is happening
10 there? We are torn between doubt, hope, joy, and despair. We have been deceived too often to be able wholeheartedly to believe in the great miracle.

Chief-of-Staff Röhm stands at the window the whole time, watching the door of the Chancellory from which the Leader
15 must emerge. We shall be able to judge by his face if the interview was happy.

Torturing hours of waiting! At last a car draws up in front of the entrance. The crowd cheers. They seem to feel that a great change is taking place or has already begun.
20 A few moments later he is with us. He says nothing, and we all remain silent also. His eyes are full of tears. It has come! The Leader is appointed Chancellor. He has already been sworn in by the President of the Reich. The final decision has been made. Germany is at a turning-point in her history. . . .

25   Indescribable enthusiasm fills the streets. A few yards from the
     Chancellory, the President of the Reich stands at his window, a
     towering, dignified, heroic figure, invested with a touch of old-
     time marvel. . . . Hundreds and thousands and hundreds of
     thousands march past our windows in never-ending, uniform
30   rhythm.
        The rising of a nation!
        Germany has awakened!
           Joseph Goebbels, *My Part in Germany's Fight* (London,
           Hutchinson Publishing Group, 1935), pp 207–8

(b) A historian's comment

No class or group or party in Germany could escape its share of
responsibility for the abandonment of the democratic Republic
35   and the advent of Adolf Hitler. The cardinal error of the Germans
who opposed Nazism was their failure to unite against it. At the
crest of their popular strength, in July 1932, the National Socialists
had attained but 37 per cent of the vote. But the 63 per cent of the
German people who expressed their opposition to Hitler were
40   much too divided and shortsighted to combine against a common
danger which they must have known would overwhelm them
unless they united, however temporarily, to stamp it out. The
Communists, at the behest of Moscow, were committed to the
last to the silly idea of first destroying the Social Democrats, the
45   Socialist trade unions and what middle-class democratic forces
there were . . .
   [T]he Third Reich owed nothing to the fortunes of war or to
foreign influence. It was inaugurated in peacetime, and peacefully,
by the Germans themselves, out of both their weaknesses and
50   their strengths. The Germans imposed the Nazi tyranny on
themselves.
           William L. Shirer, *The Rise and Fall of the Third Reich: A
           History of Nazi Germany* (London, Secker and Warburg,
           1962), pp 185–7

Questions

a   Identify (i) 'the aged President of the Reich' (lines 3–4); (ii) 'the
    great miracle' (line 12); (iii) 'the interview' (line 15); (iv) Joseph
    Goebbels, the author of extract *a*.
b   What do you think Goebbels intended to suggest by 'We are
    torn between doubt, hope, joy, and despair' (line 10)?
c   On what evidence might a contemporary in January 1933 have
    agreed with Goebbels' opinion that the National Socialists
    'have been deceived too often' (line 11)?
d   Do you find Goebbels' claim that 30 January 1933 marks 'a
    turning-point' (line 24) in the history of Germany acceptable?

★ *e* Account for the 'failure' (line 36) of 'the democratic Republic' (line 34) to unite all the Germans 'who opposed Nazism' (line 36) against the 'common danger' (lines 40–1).

★ *f* The Third Reich 'was inaugurated in peacetime, and peacefully' (line 48). Describe briefly the process by which National Socialism rose to power in Germany.

g Explain and comment briefly on the validity of Shirer's claim that 'The Germans imposed the Nazi tyranny on themselves' (lines 50–1).

h What reservations would you make in using an account, such as Goebbels' in extract *a*, as historical evidence?

5 Hitler's First Acts

(a) On the morrow of the Reichstag fire, 28 February 1933

Compose an effective placard against the Socialists and Communists. No Marxist papers are published in the whole Reich any more. Goering has initiated energetic measures in Prussia against the 'Red' parties; it will end with their complete destruction.

5   The Cabinet has issued a sharp decree against the Communist Party. This decree provides for capital punishment. This is necessary. The people demand it.

    Arrests upon arrests. Now the 'Red' pest is being thoroughly rooted out. No sign of resistance anywhere. The opponents seem

10 to be so overwhelmed by our energetic action that they dare no longer offer resistance.

    Inspect the effects of the fire in the Reichstag. The Hall of Fullsession is a sad picture of devastation. Wreckage upon wreckage. The Communist Party will have to pay for it dearly.

15 Indescribable indignation at this cowardly *attentat* is universally expressed.

    Now work proceeds smoothly. The worst is over.

        Diarised in Joseph Goebbels, op cit, *sub die*

(b) Hitler announces withdrawal from Disarmament Conference and League of Nations, 14 October 1933

Filled with the sincere desire to accomplish the work of the peaceful internal reconstruction of our nation and of its political

20 and economic life, former German Governments, trusting in the grant of a dignified equality of rights, declared their willingness to enter the League of Nations and to take part in the Disarmament Conference.

    In this connexion Germany suffered a bitter disappointment.

25   In spite of our readiness to carry through German disarmament

. . . other Governments could not decide to redeem the pledges signed by them in the Peace Treaty.

By the deliberate refusal of real moral and material equality of rights to Germany, the German nation and its Governments have
30 been profoundly humiliated.

After the German Government had declared, as a result of the equality of rights expressly laid down on December 11 1932, that it was again prepared to take part in the Disarmament Conference, the German Foreign Minister and our delegates were informed
35 . . . that this equality of rights could no longer be granted to present-day Germany.

As the German Government regards this action as an unjust and humiliating discrimination against the German nation, it is not in a position to continue, as an outlawed and second-class nation, to
40 take part in negotiations which could only lead to further arbitrary results.

While the German Government again proclaims its unshaken desire for peace, it declares to its great regret that . . . it must leave the Disarmament Conference. It will also announce its
45 departure from the League of Nations.

> *Documents on International Affairs, 1928–39, Documents 1933,*
> pp 287–9

Questions

a Who is Goering (line 3)?

b Identify and comment briefly on the 'sharp decree' which 'The Cabinet has issued . . . against the Communist Party' (lines 5–6).

★ *c* Far from being 'a Communist crime against the new government' (Papen), the Reichstag fire was a Nazi-connived plan to help Hitler stay in power. Discuss extract *a* in the light of this opinion.

★ *d* What other measures did Hitler take to crush any possible opposition to his regime?

e What were 'the pledges' (line 26)? Which 'other Governments' (line 26), according to Hitler, failed 'to redeem' them?

f Explain clearly the historical context of Hitler's reference to 'the grant of a dignified equality of rights' (lines 20–1).

g From your knowledge of the interwar period, how far, in your opinion, are Hitler's reasons in extract *b* for his withdrawal from the Disarmament Conference and the League of Nations justified?

h By 14 October 1933 'the opposition to Germany was inwardly demoralized' (Taylor). Discuss briefly Hitler's decision to withdraw from the Disarmament Conference in the light of this quotation.

i What insight does extract *b* provide into Hitler's 'method in foreign affairs'?

★ *j* What effects did Hitler's withdrawal from the Disarmament Conference and the League of Nations have on international relations?

6 The Nazis and Hitler: Two Contemporary Views

(a) Harold Nicolson on Hitlerism. Berlin, 27 January 1932

There was a moment when Hitler stood at the crest of national emotion. He could then have made either a coup d'état or forced a coalition with Brüning. He has missed that moment. The intelligent people feel that the economic situation is so complicated
5 that only experts should be allowed to deal with it. The unintelligent people are beginning to feel that Brüning and not Hitler represents the soul of Germany. In Prussia it is true Hitler is gaining ground. But he is losing it in Bavaria and Würtemberg which are comparatively prosperous. Hitlerism, as a doctrine, is a
10 doctrine of despair. I have the impression that the whole Nazi movement has been a catastrophe for this country. It has mobilised and coordinated the discontented into an expectant group: Hitlerism can never satisfy these expectations: the opinion they have mobilised may in the end swing suddenly over to
15 communism. And if that be a disaster . . . then Hitler is responsible.

> Harold Nicolson, *Diaries and Letters 1930–1964*, edited and condensed by Stanley Olson (Harmondsworth, Penguin, 1984), p 38

(b) Count Harry Kessler recalls Count Hermann Keyserling's conversation with him. Paris, 6 July 1933

[W]e sat down together on the terrace and drank a couple of bottles of champagne while Keyserling held forth most interestingly about the Nazis and Hitler. He repeated that the Nazis have a
20 much more radical revolution in mind than that of the Bolsheviks. They want to alter fundamentally the intellectual as well as the political and social structure of the German nation. It is really a religious upheaval. . . . They are in the process of abolishing Protestantism and Roman Catholicism, indeed Christianity
25 altogether, in order to effect a return to what they regard as the Old Teutonic faith. . . . According to his handwriting and physiognomy, Hitler (whom he has studied in detail) clearly falls into the potential suicide category, a man looking for death. He embodies a fundamental trait of the German nation, which has

30   always been in love with death and to whom the tribulation of the
Nibelungs is a constantly recurrent basic experience. Germans
only feel integrally German when this situation is given; they
admire and they desire purposeless death in the shape of self-
sacrifice. And they sense that through Hitler they are once more
35   being led towards grandiose destruction, a tribulation of the
Nibelungs. That is what fascinates them about him. He is fulfilling
their deepest longing. . . . Hitler is nothing, simply a medium for
the Nazi movement.

        Charles Kessler, *The Diaries of a Cosmopolitan*, pp 461–2

Questions

a   Identify the 'moment' before January 1932 when, according to
extract *a*, 'Hitler stood at the crest of national emotion' (lines
1–2). Do you agree with Nicolson that Hitler had in fact
'missed that moment' (line 3)?

b   Who is Brüning?

c   What, do you think, is Nicolson's purpose in distinguishing
between the 'intelligent' and the 'unintelligent' people in lines
3–7?

d   What do you understand by 'the Old Teutonic faith' (line 26)?
Explain the historical context of 'They are in the process of
abolishing Protestantism and Roman Catholicism' (lines 23–4).

e   'A nation comes into existence with its mythology' (Schelling).
What do you think Keyserling intended to suggest by 'Hitler is
nothing, simply a medium for the Nazi movement' (lines 37–
38)?

f   Summarise and explain the attitude of Nicolson and Keyserling
towards 'Hitlerism' as set out in both documents.

7   Hitler's Anti-Semitism

(a) Hitler's conversation with Hermann Rauschning, 1934

Two worlds face one another – the men of God and the men of
Satan! The Jew is the anti-man, the creature of another god. He
must have come from another root of the human race. I set the
Aryan and the Jew over against each other; and if I call one of
5   them a human being I must call the other something else. The two
are as widely separated as man and beast. Not that I would call the
Jew a beast. He is much further from the beasts than we Aryans.
He is a creature outside nature and alien to nature.

        Reproduced in Hermann Rauschning, *Hitler Speaks: A Series
of Political Conversations with Adolf Hitler on his Real Aims*
(London, Thornton Butterworth, February 1940), p 238.
        Hermann Rauschning was one of the Nazi leaders of the
Danzig Senate and a personal friend of Hitler

(b) Position of the Jews in Germany, 1934

10 It is very difficult to make any statement of the position of the Jews in Germany at present beyond saying that, with very few exceptions, they have disappeared from all positions of any importance in the public services, in trade and industry, from the liberal professions and the arts. Firms owned by Jews have had various fates, as have Jewish employees; there are no rules in these
15 matters, it is a question of public opinion and the immense pressure which it is able to exercise. If an Aryan staff will not work for a Jewish master, he obviously has no option but to sell the business, if customers refuse to deal with a Jewish manager or commercial traveller he obviously cannot be kept on, nobody can
20 compel the public to buy in a Jewish shop if they do not want to, but to say exactly what effect all these occurrences have had on German economy and on the Jews is clearly impossible; all one can venture on stating is that about 60,000 Jews are known to have left Germany, that the Jewish private banks have hardly been
25 interfered with at all, and that Jews in small towns and in the country generally suffer more than those in the big towns.

> *Economic Conditions in Germany to June 1934*, report by J. W. F. Thelwall (London, H.M.S.O., 1934), p 13

Questions

a To what extent, and for what reasons, was Hitler's pathological hatred of the Jew, such as illustrated in extract *a*, popular in Germany?

b What do these extracts tell us about the position of the Jews in Germany until 1934?

★ c Briefly outline the measures taken by the Nazis against the Jews *before* and *after* 1935 when the 'Nuremberg Laws' were promulgated.

d Comment on Thelwall's style as evidenced in extract *b*.

8 Foreign Policy: Hitler's Views in 1934

'The struggle against Versailles,' [Hitler] said, 'is the means, but not the end of my policy. I am not in the least interested in the former frontiers of the Reich. The re-creation of pre-war Germany is not a task worthy of our revolution.'
5 'Do you plan to attack Russia with the assistance of Poland?' I asked him. . . .
'Soviet Russia . . . is a difficult problem. I doubt if I shall be able to start anything there. . . . I have little use for a military might and a new Polish great power on my frontiers. . . . A war
10 with Russia would not be in my interest.'

In that case, I replied, Poland would hardly be likely to surrender any of her western territory.

'Then I shall force her. I have it in my power to force her to neutrality. It would be a simple matter for me to partition
15 Poland. . . . All our agreements with Poland have a purely temporary significance. I have no intention of maintaining a serious friendship with Poland. I do not need to share my power with anyone. . . . I could at any time come to an agreement with Soviet Russia . . . I could partition Poland when and how I
20 pleased. But I don't want to. It would cost too much. If I can avoid it, I will not do it. I need Poland only so long as I am still menaced by the West.'

'Do you seriously intend to fight the West?' I asked. . . .

'What else do you think we're aiming for?' he retorted.
25 I said that I thought this would surely call forth a hostile coalition against Germany which would be too strong for her.

'That is what I have to prevent. We must proceed step by step, so that no one will impede our advance. How to do this I don't yet know. But that it will be done is guaranteed by Britain's lack
30 of firmness and France's internal disunity.' . . .

I objected that we might find ourselves grievously mistaken in our belief in the impotence of Britain and France.

Hitler laughed scornfully. . . .

'Britain *needs* a strong Germany. Britain and France will never
35 again make common cause against Germany. . . . I shall do everything in my power to prevent co-operation between Britain and France. If I succeed in bringing in Italy and Britain on our side, the first part of our struggle for power will be greatly facilitated.' . . .
40 'But supposing Britain, France and Russia make an alliance?'

'That would be the end. But even if we would not conquer then, we should drag half the world into destruction with us, and leave no one to triumph over Germany. There will not be another 1918. We shall not surrender.'

Hermann Rauschning, op cit, pp 121–5

Questions

★ *a* Suggest what Hitler had in mind when he referred to 'the end of my policy' (line 2). How did he exploit the Treaty of Versailles to realise his ambitions up to 1934?

b 'Soviet Russia . . . is a difficult problem' (line 7). How serious was this 'problem' if Hitler 'could at any time come to an agreement' (line 18) with her?

c Identify 'All our agreements with Poland' (line 15).

d How much of Hitler's criticism of Britain and France in lines 29–30 seems to you to be justified? Explain fully why.

e What do you think Hitler intended to suggest by 'Britain *needs* a strong Germany' (line 34)?

★ *f* What steps did Hitler take 'to prevent co-operation between Britain and France' (lines 36–7)? What chances did he have in 1934 of 'bringing in Italy and Britain' (line 37) on Germany's side?

★ *g* From your knowledge of the period, how realistic was it to speak in terms of a possible triple alliance between France, Britain and Soviet Russia in 1934?

9 Lebensraum

(a) Hitler's view, 1934

If Germany is to become a world power, and not merely a continental state . . . then it must achieve complete sovereignty and independence. . . . Do you understand what it means? Is it not clear to you how tragically mutilated we are by the restriction
5   and hemming-in of our vital space, a restriction which condemns us to the status of a second-rate power in Europe? Only nations living independently in their own space and capable of military defence can be world powers. Only such nations are sovereign in the true sense of the word.
10   Russia is such a state . . ., the United States, Britain – but only by artificial means, not at all from the nature of its populated areas. France is such a state up to a point. Why should we be worse off? Is this an unavoidable inferiority? Is it necessary that in spite of our diligence and efficiency, in spite of our industries and
15   our military skill, we should always remain second to Britain, second to France, though we are greater than both of them together? This is why I must gain space for Germany, space big enough to enable us to defend ourselves against any military coalition. In peacetime we can manage. But in war the important
20   thing is freedom of action, for in war one is mortally dependent on the outside world. Our dependence on foreign trade without even an ocean coastline would condemn us eternally to the position of a politically dependent nation.
    We need space . . . to make us independent of every possible
25   political grouping and alliance. In the east, we must have the mastery as far as the Caucasus and Iran. In the west, we need the French coast. We need Flanders and Holland. Above all we need Sweden. We must become a colonial power. We must have a sea power equal to that of Britain. The material basis for independence
30   grows with the increasing demands of technique and armaments.

We cannot, like Bismarck, limit ourselves to national aims. We must rule Europe or fall apart as a nation, fall back into the chaos of small states. Now do you understand why I cannot be limited, either in the east or in the west?

Hitler's conversation with Hermann Rauschning, recorded in Hermann Rauschning, op cit, pp 125–6

(b) A historian's view

35 Hitler spoke most frequently and frankly about *Lebensraum* in the second half of the 1920s. . . . The arguments were pseudo-economic in nature. His starting point was the bland assumption that Germany could not possibly feed, within her present frontiers, a population of 74 millions increasing annually by 900,000. Birth

40 control . . . he flatly rejected on the ground that it would deprive Germany of her most creative intelligences. . . . Emigration was equally unacceptable to him because it robbed Germany of her best racial stock. Internal colonization had more to commend it in his eyes but only up to a point as increased yields would quickly

45 be swallowed up by rising demand. The obvious solution of increasing exports to pay for increased food imports could be dismissed as impracticable at a time of acute economic depression. Apart from that, it was militarily undesirable to make Germany too dependent on the outside world, disadvantaging her in

50 wartime. On these highly dubious premises he arrived at the only conclusion that really interested him: 'If you want to feed the German people,' he remarked, 'you must always give pride of place to the use of force. . . .

A strong case can be made out for the proposition that in power

55 the Nazi objective was not the acquisition of living space in the east to ease the pressure of population but the dismantling of the Versailles Treaty and the extension of German commercial and political control over central and southeastern Europe, to create a closed economic system supplying Germany with raw materials

60 and food and reducing her dependence on overseas imports. Even when the pace of German foreign policy quickened in 1937–8 and Hitler, returning to the theme of *Lebensraum*, spoke of the need to solve the German problem by 1943–5, he made no reference to Russia – the only country with vast empty spaces – but only to the

65 desirability of seizing Austria and Czechoslovakia as soon as possible. It almost seems as if living space had a purely symbolical quality for the Nazi Party and its leader, performing the function of 'an ideological metaphor'; a mystical *volkisch* goal . . . was being used to justify in terms of first principles the feverish pace of

70 a foreign policy directed at the attainment of rather different objectives.

William Carr, *Hitler: A Study in Personality and Politics* (London, Edward Arnold, 1978), pp 128–9

Questions

★ *a* '[H]ow tragically mutilated we are by the restriction and hemming-in of our vital space' (lines 4–5). How justified historically is Hitler's grievance?

b Explain *Lebensraum* and comment briefly on Hitler's motives as they appear in his 'conversation' with Hermann Rauschning in extract *a*.

c Summarise what extract *b* tells us about *Lebensraum* in an attempt to explain the last sentence, 'a mystical *volkisch* goal . . . objectives' (lines 68–71).

★ *d* '*Lebensraum* . . . did not drive Germany to war. Rather war, or a warlike policy, produced the demand for *Lebensraum*' (Taylor). With reference to the two extracts, comment briefly on the validity of this view.

10 Hitler's Personality

Hitler was a demonic personality obsessed by racial delusions. Physical disease is not the explanation for the weird tensions in his mind and the sudden freaks of his will. If any medical term applies to his mental state at all, it would undoubtedly be 'megalomania'.
5 But he was in no sense mentally ill; rather he was mentally abnormal, a person who stood on the broad threshold between genius and madness. . . . In mind and soul Hitler was a hybrid creature – double-faced. Ambivalence is often the concomitant of genius; inner stresses can strengthen the entire personality. But in
10 Hitler the inner contradictions had got out of hand; the split in his nature had become the determinant of his whole being. For that reason his essential nature cannot be understood in simple and natural terms; it can be grasped only as a union of opposites. Therein lies the secret of his unfathomability. It is this that makes
15 it so difficult to explain the gulf between his outward show of being a selfless servant of the nation and the monstrousness of his actions, which became obvious only in the latter part of his rule.

This fundamental dichotomy in Hitler's nature was apparent in the intellectual realm also. Hitler had extraordinary intellectual
20 gifts – in some fields undoubted genius. He had an eye for essentials, an astonishing memory, a remarkable imagination and a bold decisiveness that made for unusual success in his social undertakings and his other peaceful works. On the other hand, in many other respects – such as his treatment of the racial question,
25 his attitude towards religious matters and his astonishing underestimation of all the moral forces in life – his thinking was both primitive and cranky. These intellectual failings resulted in a frightful blindness, a fateful incapacity to deal with foreign policy

or to make the proper military decisions. In many situations he
30 could act logically. He was sensitive to nuances. He had the
intelligence and boldness to restore seven million unemployed to
places in industry. Yet at the decisive moment this same man did
not have the spark of understanding to realize that an attack on
Poland would necessarily touch off the world war which would
35 ultimately be the destruction both of himself and of Germany.
Creative intelligence and blind stupidity . . . were the outcome of
a basic abnormality. . . .

To what extent was Hitler aware of his own duality? . . . Was
he conscious that his actions were monstrous, or was he so caught
40 up in his delusions that he thought them inescapable necessities
justified by lofty ends? As I see it, his fantastically exaggerated
nationalism, his deification of the nation, was the key to his
demonic character. Hitler's unrealistic concept of the nation sprang
from his racial delusions. It is the explanation for his passionate
45 ambitions for Germany and for the inhuman crimes he did not
hesitate to commit.

Hitler considered himself a very great genius, but not a
superhuman, supernatural being. However, he viewed the nation
as supernatural, as a god whose prophetic high priest he felt
50 himself to be. He was ready to lay even the most frightful
sacrifices upon the altar of the Fatherland in order to preserve the
immortality of the nation. . . . Whatever he did for the 'higher
good of the nation' was exempted from the ordinary strictures of
conscience. In all his actions he practised the notorious principle
55 that 'the end justifies the means'. . . . His concept of 'nation' was
something quite different from the people who composed it. That
alone explains the frightful tragedy – that in the name of the
'nation' he destroyed the actual nation of which he was part.

> Otto Dietrich, *The Hitler I Knew*, trans. Richard and Clara
> Winston (London, Methuen & Co, 1957), pp 10–13.
> Written in 1946, this book was first published,
> posthumously, in 1955. Otto Dietrich joined Hitler's
> entourage in 1931, and from 1933 to 1945 'he remained an
> intimate associate of Hitler's as Reich press chief.' He died
> in 1952

Questions

a   Identify, and comment briefly on, some of Hitler's (i) 'social
    undertakings' (lines 22–3); (ii) 'peaceful works' (line 23).
b   Why, in your opinion, does Otto Dietrich call Hitler's thinking
    'both primitive and cranky' (line 27) with reference to (i) 'his
    treatment of the racial question' (line 24); (ii) 'his attitude towards
    religious matters' (line 25); (iii) 'his astonishing underestimation
    of all the moral forces in life' (lines 25–6).

c '[A] fateful incapacity' (line 28). Do you find this an objective evaluation of Hitler's approach to foreign policy?

d Explain, and comment briefly on, Hitler's (i) 'fantastically exaggerated nationalism' (lines 41–2); (ii) 'deification of the nation' (line 42).

★ e What do you understand by Hitler's 'racial delusions' (line 44)? How were these reflected in his domestic and foreign policy?

f What does this extract add to your previous knowledge of Hitler's personality?

★ g '[D]ocuments alone . . . cannot completely explain the nature of a dictatorship, or of its leaders' (Isar Verlag). In the light of this quotation, discuss the value of this extract from Dietrich's memoirs as historical evidence.

VI Rising Aggression 1935–37

Introduction

'Success and the absence of resistance,' observes Alan Bullock, 'tempted Hitler to reach out further, to take bigger risks and to shorten the intervals between his *coups*.' In October 1933 Hitler had boldly withdrawn from the League of Nations. In March 1935 he annexed the Saar and defied the Versailles Treaty by announcing general conscription and by stepping up Germany's rearmament programme. Those who sought to uphold the settlement of 1919 created what eventually turned out to be a temporary front at Stresa to condemn Hitler's first 'gamble'. Then on 7 March 1936 Hitler denounced Locarno, remilitarised the Rhineland and ordered the building of the Siegfried Line on Germany's western frontier. The French government of Albert Sarraut, 'weak and tottering to its fall', lost precious time consulting Britain and lodging protests with the League of Nations (Thomson). On her part Britain declined to offer any forcible action, lest such resistance would make Communism's access road to western Europe easier – or so Edward Halifax, British Foreign Secretary, believed. Was it not this 'conspiratorial mentality' to destroy Bolshevism that inspired the Soviet Union's policy 'of collective security and the indivisibility of peace', so uncompromisingly defended by Maxim Litvinov at Geneva? The western democracies' mistaken assumptions of the true nature of Fascist objectives made possible Hitler's stunning achievements, their apparent impotence and futility encouraged the rising tide of aggression in the 1930s.

By the time of Hitler's *coup* in the Rhineland the vacillating attitude of Britain and France was already growing into a recognisable pattern of weakness. It had already been manifested in their reluctance to wage a full-scale economic war on Fascist Italy during the Abyssinian crisis. Not only had the sanctions failed to lure Mussolini away from the Nazi sphere of influence; they made the ground more fertile for a possible *rapprochement* between the two hitherto antagonistic dictators. The *Duce* himself later confessed that '[i]f the League of Nations had followed Eden's advice in the Abyssinian dispute and had extended economic sanctions to oil, I would have had to withdraw from Abyssinia within a week. That would have been an incalculable disaster for me.'

More perhaps than the Abyssinian crisis, the Spanish Civil War drove a wedge between Mussolini and the western allies. Britain and France advocated a strict policy of non-intervention. The Republicans received help from the Soviet Union. The Fascist regimes supported the Nationalist rebels under the leadership of General Francisco Franco – Italy getting increasingly involved through her supply of arms and regular army units; Germany, whose main concern was 'to keep Italy estranged from England and France', through the provision of other war materials and technical expertise. The Spanish Civil War, writes Stavrianos, 'was essentially two wars in one – a deep-rooted social conflict generated by the decay and tensions of Spanish society, and a dress rehearsal for World War II arising from the clash of ideologies and of Great Power interests.'

In October 1936, three months after the outbreak of the war in Spain, the Rome–Berlin Axis was formed. 'The success of [the dictators'] concerted action in Spain sealed the alliance of fascism' (Thomson). In November the Anti-Comintern Pact was signed between Germany and Japan, to which Mussolini adhered on 6 November 1937. The Rome–Berlin Axis was thus converted into what Hitler defined as a 'great world-political triangle', consisting 'not of three powerless images but of three States which are prepared and determined to protect decisively their rights and vital interests.' The next month Italy withdrew from the League of Nations. 'The decision of 11 December 1937 marked the final abandonment by the Duce's Italy of the Europe of Versailles' (Lowe/Marzari).

The situation towards the end of 1937 is neatly summed up by William Carr:

> By this time the League of Nations was a completely broken reed. Power politics had returned to the forefront of international relations, and states great and small alike were adjusting themselves to the reality of a balance of power moving rapidly back to Berlin. Britain and France were driven onto the defensive. The Locarno system to which they pinned their faith lay in ruins . . . and when Belgium declared her neutrality in 1937, the strategic position of France *vis-a-vis* Germany was rendered even more serious. . . . Russia [was] racked by internal convulsions . . . while in Central Europe the Little Entente was rapidly disintegrating.

1 Maxim Litvinov, Soviet Foreign Commissar, addresses the League of Nations

We are now confronted with the task of averting war by more

effective means. The failure of the Disarmament Conference, on which formerly such high hopes were placed, in its turn compels us to seek more effective means. We must accept the incontestable fact that in the present complicated state of political and economic interests, no war of any serious dimensions can be localized and any war, whatever its issue, will turn out to have been but the first of a series. We must also tell ourselves that sooner or later any war will bring misfortune to all countries, whether belligerents or neutrals. The lesson of the World War . . . must not be forgotten. The impoverishment of the whole world, the lowering of living standards for both manual and brain workers, unemployment, the robbing of all-and-sundry of their confidence in the morrow, not to speak of the fall in cultural values, the return of some countries to medieval ideology – such are the consequences of the World War, even now, sixteen years after its cessation, making themselves acutely felt.

Finally, we must realize once and for all that no war with political and economic aims is capable of restoring so-called historical justice and that all it could do would be to substitute new and perhaps still more glaring injustices for old ones, and that every new peace treaty bears within it the seeds of fresh warfare. Further we must not lose sight of the new increase in armaments going on under our very eyes, the chief danger of which consists in its qualitative still more than in its quantitative increase, in the vast increase of potential destruction. The fact that aerial warfare has with such lightning speed won itself an equal place with land and naval warfare is sufficient corroboration of this argument. . . .

One thing is quite clear for me and that is that peace and security cannot be organised on the shifting sands of verbal promises and declarations. The nations are not to be soothed into a feeling of security by assurances of peaceful intentions, however often they are repeated, especially in those places where there are grounds for expecting aggression or where, only the day before, there have been talk and publications about wars of conquest in all directions, for which both ideological and material preparations are being made. We should establish that any State is entitled to demand from its neighbours, near and remote, guarantees for its security, and that such a demand is not to be considered as an expression of mistrust. Governments with a clear conscience and really free from all aggressive intentions, cannot refuse to give, in place of declarations, more effective guarantees which would be extended to themselves and give them also a feeling of complete security.

I am by no means overrating the opportunities and means of the League of Nations for the organization of peace. I realize, better perhaps than any of you, how limited these means are. I am aware

that the League does not possess the means for the complete
50 abolition of war.

> Reproduced in Lewis Copeland, op cit, pp 448–9

Questions

a   What internal evidence would enable you to suggest the
    probable date of Maxim Litvinov's address to the League of
    Nations?

★ b What were the ultimate objectives of the Disarmament
    Conference and why were 'such high hopes . . . placed' (line 3)
    on the realisation of these objectives? Why did the Conference
    fail?

★ c What evidence is there of a 'fall in cultural values' (line 15) during
    the inter-war period? (See Chapter II, extracts 7a and b.)

d   Explain carefully the meaning of, and comment briefly on, the
    following: (i) 'no war of any serious dimensions can be
    localized' (line 6); (ii) 'the return of some countries to medieval
    ideology' (lines 14–15); (iii) 'restoring so-called historical justice'
    (lines 19–20); (iv) 'every new peace treaty bears within it the seeds
    of fresh warfare' (line 22); (v) the 'qualitative' increase in
    armaments (line 25).

★ e From your knowledge of the period, how valid, in your
    opinion, are the author's observations in lines 32–8, 'The
    nations . . . being made'? Support your argument with cross-
    references to factual historical evidence.

f   'I realize, better perhaps than any of you' (lines 47–8). Why,
    in your opinion, should Litvinov consider himself better
    informed of the League's weaknesses than the other members?

g   What impression of Russia's position in international relations
    do you derive from this extract?

2 Hitler Abrogates Versailles Treaty, 16 March 1935

The world . . . has again resumed its cries of war, just as though
there never had been a World War nor the Versailles Treaty. In
the midst of these highly armed warlike States . . . Germany was,
militarily speaking, in a vacuum, defencelessly at the mercy of
5   every threatening danger.

The German people recall the misfortune and suffering of fifteen
years' economic misery and political and moral humiliation. It
was, therefore, understandable that Germany began loudly to
demand the fulfilment of the promises made by other States to
10 disarm. . . .

The German Government must, however, to its regret, note

that for months the rest of the world has been rearming continuously and increasingly. It sees in the creation of a Soviet Russian Army of 101 divisions, that is, in an admitted peace strength of 960,000 men, an element that at the time of the conclusion of the Versailles Treaty could not have been divined. It sees in the forcing of similar measures in other States further proofs of the refusal to accept the disarmament ideas as originally proclaimed. . . .

In these circumstances the German Government considers it impossible still longer to refrain from taking the necessary measures for the security of the Reich or even to hide the knowledge thereof from other nations. . . .

What the German Government . . . desires is to make sure that Germany possesses sufficient instruments of power not only to maintain the integrity of the German Reich, but also to command international respect and value as co-guarantor of general peace.

For in this hour the German Government renews before the German people, before the entire world, its assurance of its determination never to proceed beyond the safeguarding of German honour and the freedom of the Reich, and especially does it not intend in rearming Germany to create any instrument for warlike attack but, on the contrary, exclusively for defence and thereby for the maintenance of peace.

Documents on International Affairs, op cit, *Documents 1935*, vol i, pp 59–64

Questions

a   Explain the historical context of (i) 'The world . . . has again resumed its cries of war' (line 1); (ii) 'the promises made by other States to disarm' (lines 8–9).

b   Do you find Hitler's reasons for Germany's decision in 1935 to rearm convincing?

★ c   Discuss briefly the *real* 'circumstances' (line 20) which encouraged Hitler formally to repudiate the disarmament clauses of the Treaty of Versailles in March 1935.

3   The Abyssinian Crisis I

(a) Mussolini's demands, 31 July 1935

[T]wo essential points emerge:

(1) That the Italian Government have no intention of injuring in any way the prestige of the League of Nations or of lessening their own collaboration in the principle of collective security, since their action is directed against a State whose existence and activities have nothing to do with the principle of European collective

security. To refuse to admit this standpoint of the Italian
Government would be tantamount to a readiness to sacrifice
deliberately the interests of a State such as Italy to the application
10 of principles which in the case of Abyssinia cannot be applied. It
would, moreover, be synonymous with granting impunity to the
latter for her present action and with making it possible for her to
become an ever-growing danger in the future, merely for
defending principles of which Abyssinia avails herself to her own
15 exclusive advantage, but to which she is unable to make any . . .
contribution in the comity of the civilised nations of Europe.

(2) That it is by no means the intention of Italy to violate
existing treaties, by which she considers herself to be strictly
bound especially towards England and France, but that it is the
20 firm determination of the Italian Government not to allow these
treaties to be given an interpretation which at the present moment
would only serve to mask the military preparation of Ethiopia and
to prevent Italy from attaining that degree of security to which
she, in common with other States, is entitled in order to be in a
25 position to bring to bear on European collective security the
whole weight and force of her collaboration.

> Mussolini's communication to Sir Eric Drummond, British
> Ambassador to Italy, reproduced in C. J. Lowe & F.
> Marzari, *Italian Foreign Policy 1870–1940* (London, Routledge
> & Kegan Paul, 1975), pp 404–5

(b) Haile Selassie's appeal to the democracies, 13 September 1935

Five months before the pretext found in December in the Wal-Wal
incident, Italy had begun the armament of her colonies, armament
which since has been intensified and increased by the continuous
30 sending of troops, mechanized equipment and ammunition during
the entire duration of the work of the Council of the League of
Nations and the work of the arbitration board.

Now that the pretext on which they planned to make war upon
us has vanished, Italy, after having obtained from the powers their
35 refusal to permit us to purchase armaments and ammunition
which we do not manufacture and which are necessary to our
defence, seeks to discredit the Ethiopian people and their
government before world opinion.

They characterize us as a barbarous people whom it is necessary
40 to civilize. The attitude of Italy will be judged by history. We will
see whether it is the act of a nation that prides herself as being the
epitome of civilization to make an unjust attack on a pacific
people, recently disarmed and which placed all their confidence in
her promise of peace and friendship which the civilized nation had
45 previously given in a treaty made on her own initiative seven
years before, to be exact, August 2, 1928. . . .

Our delegation at Geneva has received our formal instructions
to demand of the Council of the League of Nations the institution
of an international commission of inquiry. . . .
50   We do not want war. Ethiopia puts her confidence in God. . . .
She wishes and hopes . . . that an amicable and peaceful
settlement, in accordance with right and justice, will intervene,
and the officers of the Council of the League of Nations, in
conformity with the pact, will compel all the nations of the world,
55   great and small, who hold peace as their ideal, to halt this crisis
which threatens to stop all civilization.
Reproduced in Lewis Copeland, op cit, pp 450–1

Questions

a   Explain the historical context of (i) 'the principle of collective
security' (line 4); (ii) Abyssinia's 'present action' (line 12);
(iii) 'existing treaties' (line 18) binding Italy 'especially towards
England and France' (line 19).

b   Do you find the Italian Government's 'standpoint' (line 8) as
expounded by Mussolini in extract *a* acceptable?

c   Identify (i) Haile Selassie; (ii) 'the Wal-Wal incident' (lines
27–8); (iii) 'the work of the arbitration board' (line 32); (iv) 'a
treaty' (line 45).

★   d   Account for the failure of the League to 'compel all the nations
of the world . . . to halt this crisis' (lines 54–5).

e   What other sources would you consult to assess objectively the
claims of both contestants as given in extracts *a* and *b*?

4   The Abyssinian Crisis II

(a) *A tale of sin and nemesis*

From an English standpoint the Mussolinian sin of commission –
the positive, strong-willed, aggressive egotism which had tempted
the Italian war-lord into committing a crime of violence in breach
of all his covenants . – was inextricably interwoven with a
5   complementary sin of omission: a negative, weak-willed, cowardly
egotism which had tempted the reigning politicians in Great
Britain and France – in deference to what they believed to be the
will of their constituents – to stop short of an effective fulfilment
of their own covenants because they flinched from the risks and
10   sacrifices to which their countries stood pledged to expose
themselves in the cause of international justice and law and order.
While Signor Mussolini had not the patience and imagination to
abide by his promises to promote Italy's legitimate national
interests by none other than peaceful means, his French and
15   British fellow actors had not the virtues requisite for whole-

heartedly putting into practice the nobler and wiser policy to which they were paying, all the time, a perfunctory lip service. Their professed intention . . . was to establish a reign of law and order in the international arena by making a reality of both the
20 twin pillars of Justice: Collective Security and Peaceful Change. Yet when their sincerity was put to a supreme test through an Italian challenge . . . in the seventeen post-war years that ended in 1935, the French and English did not muster up either the generosity and imagination to make a success of Peaceful Change
25 or the courage and imagination to make a success of Collective Security. They neither responded in 1920 to Signor Tittoni's plea for an equitable distribution of raw materials nor restrained by Signor Mussolini in 1935 from launching an aggressive war against Abyssinia.
30 In this light it is apparent that the sin which was committed in 1935 was not merely Mussolini's or Fascismo's or Italy's. This guilt was shared by Britain and France, and in some measure by the whole living generation of the Western Society.

> Arnold J. Toynbee, *Survey of International Affairs 1935*, vol ii (London, 1936). Reproduced in *The Ethiopian Crisis: Touchstone of Appeasement?*, ed. Ludwig F. Schaefer (Massachusetts, D.C. Heath & Co, 1961), p 18

(b) A deathblow to the League

The real death of the League was in December 1935, not in 1939
35 or 1945. One day it was a powerful body imposing sanctions, seemingly more effective than ever before; the next day it was an empty sham, everyone scuttling from it as quickly as possible. What killed the League was the publication of the Hoare–Laval plan. Yet this was a perfectly sensible plan, in line with the
40 League's previous acts of conciliation from Corfu to Manchuria. It would have ended the war; satisfied Italy; and left Abyssinia with a more workable, national territory. The commonsense of the plan was, in the circumstances of the time, its vital defect. For the League action against Italy was not a commonsense extension of
45 practical policies; it was a demonstration of principle pure and simple. No concrete 'interest' was at stake in Abyssinia – not even for Italy: Mussolini was concerned to show off Italy's strength, not to acquire the practical gains . . . of Empire. The League powers were concerned to assert the Covenant, not to defend
50 interests of their own. The Hoare–Laval plan seemed to show that principle and practical policy could not be combined. The conclusion was false: every statesman of any merit combines the two, though in varying proportions. But everyone accepted it in 1935. . . .
55 The Abyssinian affair had more immediate effects. Hitler

watched the conflict with sharp eyes, fearful that a triumphant League might next be used against Germany, yet eager to drive a wedge between Italy and her two former partners in the Stresa front. . . . When the [Hoare–Laval] plan failed and Italian arms
60 began to succeed, Hitler resolved to exploit the breakdown of the Stresa front. At least this seems the most likely explanation for his decision to reoccupy the demilitarized Rhineland, though at present there is no solid evidence of what was in his mind.

A. J. P. Taylor, op cit, pp 96–7

Questions

a Explain briefly in your own words, and assess the historical validity of, the first sentence (lines 1–11) of extract a.

b '[A] perfunctory lip service' (line 17). Is this a fair assessment of the French and British attitude to Mussolini's 'fellow actors' (line 15) to have reacted the way they did?

c Identify Signor Tittoni (line 26) and explain the historical context of his 'plea for an equitable distribution of raw materials' (lines 26–7).

d In your study of the origins of the Second World War, what importance would you give to Toynbee's judgement in the last paragraph of extract a?

e What was the 'Hoare–Laval plan' mentioned in lines 38–9, and what, according to Taylor, were its advantages? In what ways did it reflect the League's 'previous acts of conciliation' (line 40)?

★ f Why did the Hoare–Laval plan fail?

★ g Comment briefly on the effects of 'the Abyssinian *debâcle*' (E. H. Carr) on world peace.

5   The Military on the Ascendant

(a) 'Deutsch Wehr' (a German military paper), January 1936

The twentieth century will be called, by the historians of to-morrow, the Century of War. . . . Formerly, and particularly in the 'bourgeois' age which is coming, in our time, irrevocably to its end, war used to mean an interruption, an incident in the life of
5 peace. . . . Since the catastrophe of 1914, that conception has been radically transformed. . . . A new world has been born . . . in which war is the major premiss and the measure of all things, and the military becomes the master and the legislator. . . . Peace must submit to the requirements of war, which has become the hidden
10 ruler of the century and is reducing peace to the rank of a mere armistice. . . .

This emancipation of war, the dominant event and characteristic

of our time, demands . . . the replacement of a social order based
on the principle of peace by one adapted to the needs of war. . . .
15 Every activity within society . . . will serve . . . the requirements
of the preparation or execution of war. . . . Every citizen will be a
State servant, working directly for the purposes of war. . . . War
and its execution will make up the only content of existence.

(b) Sir Austen Chamberlain, 14 February 1936

It does not now suffice to have the best Army and the best
20 General Staff or the best Navy and the best Board of Admiralty.
Modern warfare is an affair of nations, not of armies and navies,
and you have got to co-ordinate not merely the three forces but to
co-ordinate the whole of the civil activities of the population.

> Both excerpts quoted in Jonathan Griffin (one-time editor
> of *Essential News*), *Alternative to Rearmament* (London,
> Macmillan, 1936), pp 89–91

Questions

a Comment briefly on the historical validity of 'the "bourgeois"
   age which is coming . . . irrevocably to its end' (lines 3–4).
b 'The traditional distinction between soldier and civilian . . .
   disappeared' (Michael Howard). From the evidence suggested
   in these extracts, explain briefly the close interdependence of
   the military and civil 'activities of the population' (line 23)
   in Germany, Italy, Russia and Japan. How did the western
   democracies respond to this new militarism?
★ c On what evidence would you describe the interwar period as
   marked by 'an acceptance of the values of the military
   subculture as the dominant values of society' (Howard)?

6 Hitler's Break with Locarno

(a) The Nazis remilitarise the Rhineland, 7 March 1936

Germany no longer feels bound by the Locarno Treaty. In the
interests of the primitive rights of its people to the security of their
frontier and the safeguarding of their defence, the German
government has re-established, as from today, the absolute
5 and unrestricted sovereignty of the Reich in the demilitarized
zone. . . .
   In this historic hour, when, in the Reich's western provinces,
German troops are at this minute marching into their future
peacetime garrisons, we all unite in two sacred vows. . . .
10 First, we swear to yield to no force whatever in restoration of
the honour of our people. . . . Secondly, we pledge that now,

more than ever, we shall strive for an understanding between the European peoples, especially for one with our Western neighbour nations. . . . We have no territorial demands to make in Europe! 15 . . . Germany will never break the peace!

> Hitler's speech diarised in William L. Shirer, *End of a Berlin Diary* (New York, 1947), pp 51–4, reproduced in William L. Shirer, *The Rise and Fall of the Third Reich*, pp 291–2

(b) Dr K. Krofta, Czechoslovak Foreign Minister, addresses Prague Parliament, 17 March 1936

No slight matter is at stake. The Locarno Treaty of 1925, alongside the Covenant, was the pillar of European security, and on its observance and efficacy were based the hopes of all the European States that desire peace. . . . As far as we are concerned, it is 20 obvious that a State to which respect for international obligations and their unconditional fulfilment has always been a basic principle of foreign policy cannot but take a decisive stand against all unilateral breaches of treaties. . . . Our own attitude is determined by our fidelity to contractual obligations, the validity of which we 25 wish to maintain, and also by fidelity to our allies. . . . We do not wish and shall not try to escape the tasks and sacrifices arising out of membership of the League and of our treaties with our allies. . . . The Czechoslovak Republic sincerely desires peace for itself and for others. It would deeply regret if its good neighbourly 30 relations with Germany were to be seriously endangered by that country's latest unfortunate act. . . . It is necessary to build up still further our economic, military, and material forces, and to remain politically united and firm, true to the foreign policy we have hitherto pursued.

> Extract reproduced in Robert Machray, *The Struggle for the Danube and the Little Entente 1929–1938* (London, Allen & Unwin, 1938), pp 214–5

(c) An American comment

35 Neither France nor Great Britain moved.

The French government, although prodded by French public opinion to take action, was weak and vacillating. It consulted London. The British government was confronted by its own public opinion, which felt quite differently from that of France. 40 To the British people in general, all that was involved was the occupation by the German government of territory that was formerly German. Like the American people, they did not see that if the Western powers failed to prevent Hitler from carrying out his plans, the Treaty of Versailles would be destroyed and the 45 League of Nations would be tacitly admitting that Germany could defy the whole of Europe at any time in the future, whenever she felt powerful enough. Such a failure constituted a welcome notice to Hitler that he might continue with impunity upon his forward march.

50   Hitler now threw all caution to one side. Military rearmament was no longer surreptitious. . . . The German four-year-plan immediately carried into effect a consolidated civil and military organization. It prepared Germany for the outbreak of war. . . .

> Sumner Welles, *The Time for Decision* (London, Hamish Hamilton, reprint, 1945), p 30.
> The book was first published in October 1944

Questions

a   'Germany no longer feels bound by the Locarno Treaty' (line 1). Account for Hitler's decision to remilitarise the Rhineland on 7 March 1936. How valid are Hitler's reasons for this decision?

★ b   '[W]e shall strive for an understanding . . . with our Western neighbour nations' (lines 12–14). What steps did Hitler take to realise his second 'sacred' pledge?

c   'Neither France nor Great Britain moved' (line 35). Do you find Sumner Welles' assessment of the British and French reaction in extract *c* justifiable?

★ d   What was Belgium's attitude to Hitler's break with Locarno?

e   Explain and comment briefly on 'The German four-year-plan' (line 51).

★ f   'Hitler had lost more than he gained by his Rhineland *coup*' (Grenville). Consider the general consequences of Hitler's decision in the light of this quotation.

★ g   'No slight matter is at stake' (line 16). Why should Czechoslovakia be so preoccupied as a result of Hitler's break with Locarno?

h   To what extent and in what ways did Germany's 'latest unfortunate act' (line 31) alter the political situation in central and eastern Europe?

7   The Spanish Civil War

(a) Franco's Manifesto of Las Palmas

Spaniards! . . .

The situation in Spain is becoming more critical with every day that passes; anarchy reigns in most of her villages and fields; government-appointed authorities preside over the revolts, when 5   they are not actually fomenting them. Differences are settled by pistol-shots and with machine-guns among the mobs of

townspeople, who . . . kill each other, without the public
authorities imposing peace and justice.

Revolutionary strikes of all kinds are paralysing the life of the
10 nation, dissipating and destroying its sources of wealth, and
creating a state of hunger that will drive working men to
desperation.

Our monuments and artistic treasures are the object of the most
virulent attacks from revolutionary hordes obeying orders which
15 they receive from foreign elements. . . .

Emergency regulations merely serve to muzzle the people and
ensure that Spain ignores what is happening outside the gates of
her towns and cities, as well as to imprison her presumed political
adversaries.

20 The Constitution, suspended and impaired for all, is suffering a
total eclipse. . . .

To the revolutionary and unheeding spirit of the masses hoaxed
and exploited by the Soviet agents who veil the bloody reality of
that régime which sacrificed twenty-five million people in order
25 to exist, are joined the maliciousness and negligence of authorities
of all kinds, who, sheltered by a crippled power, lack the authority
and prestige.

Can we consent one day longer to the shameful spectacle we are
presenting to the world? . . .

30 Justice and Equality before the law we offer you; peace and love
between Spaniards. Liberty and Fraternity without libertinage and
tyranny. Work for all. Social justice . . . and an equitable and
progressive distribution of wealth without destroying or jeopardizing
the Spanish economy. . . .

35 Spaniards: Long live Spain!
Long live the honourable Spanish people!

Commanding General of the Canary Islands,
Santa Cruz de Tenerife, at 5.15 a.m., 18 July 1936.

Reproduced in Brian Crozier, *Franco: A Biographical History*
(London, Eyre & Spottiswoode, 1967), pp 519–22

(b) Ulrich von Hassell, German Ambassador to Rome, reports to the Wilhelmstrasse, December 1936

The role played by the Spanish conflict as regards Italy's relations
40 with France and England could be similar to that of the Abyssinian
conflict, bringing out clearly the actual, opposing interests of the
powers and thus preventing Italy from being drawn into the net of
the Western powers and used for their machinations. The struggle
for dominant political influence in Spain lays bare the natural
45 opposition between Italy and France; at the same time the position
of Italy as a power in the western Mediterranean comes into
competition with that of Britain. All the more clearly will Italy

recognize the advisability of confronting the Western powers shoulder to shoulder with Germany.

> Quoted in William L. Shirer, *The Rise and Fall of the Third Reich*, op cit, p 298

Questions

a   Identify (i) Franco; (ii) 'foreign elements' (line 15).
b   Explain the historical background to lines 20–1.
c   In what ways did 'Soviet agents' (line 23) hoax and exploit 'the revolutionary and unheeding spirit of the masses' (line 22)?
d   Do you find Franco's view of the Spanish Civil War convincing? What other contemporary sources would you use to verify his impressions?
e   How did 'the Spanish conflict' effect 'Italy's relations with France and England' (lines 39–40)? What were Germany's interests in the war?
★ f   'The struggle for dominant political influence in Spain' (lines 43–4). To what extent was the Spanish Civil War an expression of contemporary European politics?
★ g   Assess briefly the importance of the Spanish conflict in your study of the origins of the Second World War.

8   The Great World-Political Triangle

(a) *Mussolini on the Rome–Berlin Axis*

(i) *1 November 1936*: This Rome–Berlin line is not a diaphragm but an axis, around which can revolve all those European states with a will to collaboration and peace.

> Cited in Alan Cassels, *Fascist Italy* (London, Routledge & Kegan Paul, 1969), p 90

(ii) *28 September 1937, Berlin*: There are no secret intentions hidden
5   behind my visit to Germany. Nothing will be planned here to divide a Europe which is already divided enough. The solemn confirmation of the fact and stability of the Rome–Berlin axis is not directed against other States. We National-Socialists and Fascists want peace which does not silently ignore, but solves, the
10   questions arising from the life of the peoples.

> Reproduced in C. J. Lowe & F. Marzari, *Italian Foreign Policy 1870–1940* (London, Routledge & Kegan Paul, 1975), p 407

(b) *The Anti-Comintern Pact, 25 November 1936*

The Government of the German Reich and the Imperial Japanese Government:

In recognition of the fact that the aim of the Communist International . . . is the disintegration of, and the commission of
15 violence against, existing States with all means at its command;

In the conviction that the toleration of interference by the Communist International in the domestic affairs of nations not only endangers their internal peace and social welfare, but also threatens world peace;
20 Desiring to co-operate for defence against Communist disintegration, have agreed . . .

1. to keep one another informed concerning counter-measures and to carry out the latter in close collaboration.

2. jointly to invite third States whose internal peace is menaced by
25 the disintegrating work of the Communist International to adopt defensive measures in the spirit of the present agreement or to participate in the present agreement.

British and Foreign State Papers, vol cxl (1936), pp 529–30

(c) The Rome–Berlin–Tokyo Axis, 6 November 1937

We signed the [Anti-Comintern] Pact this morning. One was conscious of an atmosphere definitely unlike that of the usual
30 diplomatic ceremony. Three nations are embarking together upon a path which may perhaps lead them to war. A war necessary in order to break through the crust which is stifling the energy and the aspirations of the young nations. . . . The situation of 1935 has been transformed. Italy has broken out of her isolation: she is in
35 the centre of the most formidable political and military combination which has ever existed.

Diarised by Count Galeazzo Ciano, Italian Foreign Minister.
Reproduced in C. J. Lowe & F. Marzari, op cit, pp 407–8

(d) Churchill's comment

Once Hitler's Germany had been allowed to rearm without active interference by the Allies and former associated Powers, a second World War was almost certain. . . . The battle for peace which
40 could, during 1935, have been won, was now almost lost. . . . [Mussolini] was now bitterly estranged from us, and had joined hands with Hitler. The Berlin–Rome Axis was in being. There was now, as it turned out, little hope of averting war or of postponing it by a trial of strength equivalent to war. Almost all
45 that remained open to France and Britain was to await the moment of the challenge and do the best they could.

Winston S. Churchill, op cit, p 148

Questions

a Identify and comment briefly on the historical significance of

(i) 'my visit to Germany' (line 5); (ii) 'the Communist International' (lines 13–14); (iii) 'The situation of 1935' (line 33).

b Do you find Mussolini's definition of the Rome–Berlin Axis (extract *a* i) and the purpose behind it (extract *a* ii) convincing? Explain the historical circumstances in which the Axis was formed.

★ c To what extent was the Anti–Comintern Pact the result of a genuine fear of Communism? How far was Stalinist Russia in 1936 a real threat to 'world peace' (line 19)? What other factors, in your opinion, contributed to the formation of the Pact?

d 'Action to gain satisfaction for the unsatisfied Powers grew imminent' (E. H. Carr). In the light of this quotation, what consideration, do you think, influenced Rome, Berlin and Tokyo to embark 'together upon a path which may perhaps lead them to war' (lines 30–1)?

e From your knowledge of the period, how far do you consider Churchill's fears in extract *d* well-founded? How far is his 'comment' based on the benefit of hindsight?

VII   The Imminence of War: 'Anschluss', Munich and Appeasement

Introduction

'German-Austria must be restored to the great German Motherland.' That is how Hitler expressed his idea of *Anschluss* in 1924, giving it pride of place on the first page of *Mein Kampf*. 'People of the same blood should be in the same Reich.' He considered union with Austria his 'great task' and his first attempt at realising it was made shortly after he became Chancellor. The Nazi *Putsch* of 1934, during which Engelbert Dollfuss was murdered, failed. It cost Hitler 'a gratuitous humiliation'. Mussolini's firm posture in favour of Austrian independence had stymied the expansionist ambition of his recent guest in Venice.

In 1938 things were different. Since the establishment of the Rome-Berlin Axis late in 1936 the Fascist dictator had been absorbed within the powerful spell of the *Führer*'s personality. He was, moreover, alienated by his deep involvement in Mediterranean affairs. The pathetic state of French politics could hardly be expected to offer even the semblance of resistance. In London Neville Chamberlain's policy was one of peace and conciliation – whatever the price. Was Hitler right when, with Faustian undertones, he defined parliamentary democracy as 'an abortion of filth and fire, the creative fire of which, however, seems to have died out'? On 12 March 1938 German troops marched into Austria. Two days later, in Vienna, Hitler formally proclaimed his *Anschluss* with Austria. It was a foretaste of what was to follow. 'Vienna,' remarks Neville Henderson, British ambassador in Berlin, 'constituted Hitler's first step outside the Reich along the path of violence.'

Hitler's next objective was the dismemberment of Czechoslovakia. But the coup this time was not to be carried out by the *Führer* alone. After months of mounting tension, violent disorder and 'wild tales of Czech atrocities' in the Sudeten lands which, Hitler promised, would be his last territorial claim in Europe, Chamberlain and Daladier assembled together with Mussolini and Hitler at Munich to sign what eventually turned out to be the partition of Czechoslovakia. Instead of intensifying pressure on the aggressor, Britain and France had chosen – for the sake of peace and stability (and perhaps for time) – to sacrifice 'a far-away country'.

> I was near the German frontier [recalls Sumner Welles in *Where are we Heading?*] in the early days of September, 1938, just prior to Munich, and I heard over the radio that hysterical diatribe of hate and of rage which Hitler launched against Dr. Beneš to the Reichstag. I can still hear the gross insults levelled, as by a drunkard or a maniac, against the small, composed figure who was the President of the neighbouring state. Deserted by France and by England, Dr. Beneš was forced to resign his office a few weeks later.

Sudetenland was thus severed from Czechoslovakia which, in Hitler's sick mind, had been 'the arch-fiend which threatened the independence of the Reich' (Henderson). To the western democracies Hitler's racial ambitions appeared 'satisfied' and war was comfortably delayed for another year. In Chamberlain's view Munich meant 'peace in our time'. It was a temporary expedient. Henderson was right when he warned his Prime Minister that '[o]ceans of ink will flow hereafter in criticism of your action.' Of Chamberlain, Harold Nicolson wrote: 'no man in history has made such persistent and bone-headed mistakes'. To Churchill Munich was 'a defeat without a war . . . an awful milestone in our history' produced by a shocking lack of 'moral health and martial vigour'. In both Britain and France, however, public opinion welcomed the agreement 'with relief and jubilation'.

Why did Britain and France choose to appease the Fascist dictators? 'The options of foreign policy,' says Maurice Vaisse, 'were the extension and echoes of internal policy.' What major domestic considerations influenced the British and French decision-making process? What other objective factors advocated international detente? How fair is it to define appeasement as 'a policy of concessions designed to placate Germany and Italy'? Churchill calls the 1930s 'a line of milestones to disaster', 'a catalogue of surrenders'. To what extent was the advocacy of appeasement prompted by basic misconceptions which British and French cabinets entertained of Hitler and Mussolini? Did Britain and France have the *will* and the necessary *means* to embark on a 'preventive war'? Appeasement has generally been discredited on the grounds that it failed to prevent the outbreak of war in 1939. On what historical evidence, however, can it be assumed that had the western democracies acted differently, had they taken more 'stern and effective measures', the catastrophe would have been avoided? The war came when appeasement had in fact been almost completely abandoned.

1 France's Ideological Conflict

The crisis of May–June 1936 terrorised a great section of the French bourgeoisie. It made many of us lose sight of the dangers of Hitlerism and fascism . . . because behind the Popular Front one saw the spectre of Bolshevism. Therein lies the origin of the
5 slogans that disfigured the soul of the nation: 'Better Hitler than Stalin' and 'Why die for Danzig?'

> General Gamelin, Chief of the General Staff, in his *Servir*, vol ii (Paris, 1947), p 219. Quoted in Anthony Adamthwaite, *France and the Coming of the Second World War 1936–1939* (London, Frank Cass, 1977), p 14

Questions

a Identify the 'crisis of May–June 1936' in France and explain the historical significance of the first sentence.

★ *b* What is 'the Popular Front' (line 3)? Account for the origin of such 'slogans' (line 5) as 'Better Hitler than Stalin' and 'Why die for Danzig?' (lines 5–6).

★ *c* In 1936 'France's prestige was lower than at any other period in the interwar years' (Adamthwaite). Discuss briefly the impact of France's ideological conflict on her 'international attitudes' in the light of this quotation.

2 Thirst for Revenge

The world to-day is faced with a Germany just like that of 1914, but plus a thirst for revenge. Germany is just as ready for war, just as prepared, obedient, disciplined, armed as she was twenty-five years ago. But at that time she was a flourishing, rich nation,
5 industrious and inventive, sabre-brandishing but still sociable, so that the people could only be moved to action by the assertion that their country had been attacked by others. To-day, on the contrary, she is a nation which feels strong, and at the same time maltreated, born to rule but maliciously cheated out of victory.
10 To-day she stands in clanking armour before the world and demands requital. For this reason the Germans are so much more dangerous, because they are fighting not for self-preservation but for the restoration of what they call their honour.

It is not raw materials that the Germans want, nor yet colonies
15 nor Russian cornfields. They do not want war in order to mine their own oil or plant their own cotton. They want something much more dangerous, something which I might almost call idealistic. They want to revenge themselves for the crimes which the world committed, first when it took them by surprise at the
20 time of peace, secondly when it deceived them in signing an

oppressive Treaty, although, surrounded by enemies, they had suggested reconciliation and discussion, and finally when it forbade them weapons. . . .

War is approaching because nothing which can be bought or given will satisfy the German claim. . . . Nothing anyone could give them would satisfy them; it must be won by conquest; the Germans do not want territory, they want victory.

And this victory can only be attained in Paris. But where they will begin the war, they themselves do not yet know. . . .

The finest legends of the Germans, their songs, their stories and their wine, all come from the West, near the Rhine. It is the only land holy to all German patriots, and though it was not actually taken away from them, it was neutralized. Who imposed this shame upon them? The French. No one realizes that, but for Wilson's intervention, the left bank of the Rhine would have been French; that the Germans, in their plans for victory, intended to retain all the occupied country, or that the French could have taken anything they wished away from downtrodden Germany. But the monstrous conditions which Germany imposed at the end of 1917 on conquered Russia and Rumania, do not justify the mistakes of the Paris Treaties.

The scene in the Hall of Mirrors at Versailles is branded on the mind of every German schoolchild in burning words. It has given them a feeling of inferiority from which they must free themselves at any price. There, in Versailles, stood Bismarck once and formed the German Reich on French soil. . . .

And now in the same Hall of Mirrors a Tiger sat and compelled two poor German citizens to sign a Treaty which would take away their military arms. . . .

It is that scene at Versailles which is leading us towards a new war. The Germans see pitiful images in the mirrors of that gallery; the old victorious ones and the new annihilating ones. It is this Hall of Mirrors which every young German wants to conquer. The German Chancellor dreams of standing one day between these mirrors and of dictating the terms of peace to Clemenceau's successor. That has become the great demand of national honour, and for five years the German men, women and children have been undergoing instruction which has this revenge as its ultimate aim.

Emil Ludwig, *A New Holy Alliance*, translated from the German by David Game (London, Robert Hale Ltd, 1938), pp 49–53.
'Emil Ludwig enjoyed a great vogue during the twenties as the author of popular biographies. In the English-speaking world *Napoleon* was his best-known work, but in Germany he ensured his reputation with *Bismarck*' (Charles Kessler)

a Compare and contrast the Germany of 1914 with the Germany of 1938.

b Explain the historical context of Emil Ludwig's reference to (i) 'raw materials' (line 14); (ii) 'colonies' (line 14); (iii) 'Russian cornfields' (line 15).

c '[T]he crimes which the world committed' (lines 18–19) against the Germans. Identify and briefly comment on the circumstances when 'the world' (i) 'took them by surprise at the time of peace' (lines 19–20); (ii) 'deceived them in signing an oppressive Treaty' (lines 20–1); (iii) 'forbade them weapons' (lines 22–3).

d 'It is that scene at Versailles which is leading us towards a new war' (lines 50–1). Do you find Ludwig's arguments justifying Germany's thirst for revenge convincing?

3   Anschluss or the Rape of Austria

(a) *Extract from a semi-official Prague paper, 1936*

It would be well if France and England recognized the fact that the old, well-known attitude of the Little Entente against a Habsburg restoration remains unchanged and irrevocable. We do not ask the aid of anyone; our own powers are adequate. But it is necessary
5   seriously to draw attention to the fact that to play with the idea of a Habsburg restoration is to play with fire, and only provides assistance for the endeavours of Germany to seize Austria. It is impossible to call it anything else but nonsense to suppose that Yugoslavia would calmly accept the prospect of Germany
10   becoming an immediate neighbour; she is very well aware how Pan-Germanism, fired and strengthened by the occupation of Austria, would threaten her. Yugoslavia is just as much to be relied on in opposing *Anschluss* as are Rumania and Czechoslovakia. But this question is not a matter only for the Little Entente. It is
15   always useful to speak clearly. Should Italy, France and England inactively watch the execution of *Anschluss*, the Little Entente States could not risk their countries in a bloody and unequal fight with Germany. If the Western Great Powers, however, decide to oppose Anschluss definitively by every means, the Little Entente
20   will be no less decided.

Whether it is a matter of the policy of the Little Entente with regard to the League of Nations, the problem of the independence of Austria, the Habsburg question, the problem of changes of frontiers, the question of respect for treaty obligations, or the
25   relation of the three States to individual Great Powers or any State whatsoever, that policy is based on homogeneous principles, equal joint interests, and will be conducted by joint methods.

Reproduced in Robert Machray, op cit, p 221

(b) The aims of 'Anschluss'

The annexation of Austria was the beginning of the Third Reich's great campaign against Europe. After it no mention was made in
30 the German military papers of 'the national liberation of our Austrian brothers,' but merely of how immediately to exploit the newly won strategic positions for the preparation of a great European war.

The *Anschluss* was in the first place strategically necessary for
35 the military organization of the German–Italian alliance and for the development of the Axis. In this connection the *Militaerwochenblatt* [an Army publication] wrote with great frankness: 'The fact that Germany has now become the immediate neighbour of her friend Italy with a common frontier more than 300 kilometres long, is of
40 very great military importance. The strategic and military-economic value of this common frontier is obvious: by using all their means of transport both troops and convoys will be able to be employed to the best advantage for the strategy and war economy of both allies.' The second object of the *Anschluss* was
45 the deep break-through towards South-East Europe and the formation of a military alliance of the Southern European states under the leadership of Germany. In this connection *Militaerwochenblatt* wrote: 'From now on [since the *Anschluss*] military co-operation has become possible between Germany and
50 all the states of South-East Europe, such as Hungary, Yugoslavia, Bulgaria and even Rumania. This gives the strategic front of South-East Europe the strength and depth it requires.' The third object of annexing Austria was to enable Germany to dominate the trade of the entire southeast. As the *Militaerwochenblatt* puts it:
55 'Of particular importance, mainly for our military economy, is the fact that Germany now marches with Yugoslavia and Hungary, countries rich in raw materials and agriculturally very productive. Besides what Hungary and Yugoslavia can supply to Germany . . . supplies could also come, if necessary, from the other Balkan
60 countries – Rumania, Bulgaria, Greece and Turkey.'

Eugene Lennhoff, *X-Ray of Europe* (London, Hutchinson, 1939), pp 68–9

Questions

a Identify the 'Little Entente' (line 2). When and why was it created? Briefly explain the reference to 'a Habsburg restoration' in lines 2–3.

b What were the 'homogeneous principles' (line 26) underlying the Little Entente's opposition to *Anschluss*?

c What evidence is there to justify the Little Entente's fears in 1936 that Italy, France and Britain might 'inactively watch the execution of Anschluss' (line 16)? Why should the Little

Entente States feel so dependent upon the decisions of the western Powers?

d Summarise in your own words the aims of *Anschluss* as given in extract *b*. What German aspirations, other than those mentioned in the extract, did *Anschluss* realise?

★ *e* 'Austria has ceased to be not only a country, but also a state' (Lennhoff). What measures did the Third Reich take to reorganise Austria into 'a military centre for communications and trade'?

★ *f* Consider Lennhoff's view that Austria (now rechristened 'the Ostmark') constituted a potential source of 'internal political crisis of the Third Reich'.

4 A telephone conversation between Hitler and Prince Philip of Hesse, Hitler's special envoy to the Duce

Hesse: I have just come back from Palazzo Venezia. The Duce accepted the whole thing in a very friendly manner. He sends you his regards. He had been informed from Austria, von Schuschnigg gave him the news. He had then said it [i.e., Italian intervention]
5   would be a complete impossibility; it would be a bluff; such a thing could not be done. So he [Schuschnigg] was told that it was unfortunately arranged thus, and it could not be changed any more. Then Mussolini said that Austria would be immaterial to him.
10 *Hitler:* Then please tell Mussolini I will never forget him for this.
Hesse: Yes.
Hitler: Never, never, never, whatever happens. I am still ready to make a quite different agreement with him.
Hesse: Yes, I told him that too.
15 *Hitler:* As soon as the Austrian affair has been settled, I shall be ready to go with him through thick and thin; nothing matters.
Hesse: Yes, my Fuehrer.
Hitler: Listen, I will make any agreement – I am no longer in fear of the terrible position which would have existed militarily in case
20 we had become involved in a conflict. You may tell him that I do thank him ever so much; never, never shall I forget that.
Hesse: Yes, my Fuehrer.
Hitler: I will never forget it, whatever may happen. If he should ever need any help or be in any danger, he can be convinced that I
25 shall stick to him whatever might happen, even if the whole world were against him.
Hesse: Yes, my Fuehrer.

This conversation was 'quoted in evidence at Nuremberg'.
Reproduced in Winston S. Churchill, op cit, p 210

Questions

a   Identify (i) Palazzo Venezia (line 1); (ii) 'the whole thing' (line 2); (iii) von Schuschnigg (line 3).

b   Explain and comment briefly on the historical context of Hitler's reference to 'the terrible position . . . conflict' in lines 19–20.

★ c   'In 1934, Mussolini objected strenuously to *Anschluss*, and even threatened to invade Austria to prevent it' (Alan Cassels). So why was '[Italian intervention] . . . a complete impossibility' (lines 4–5) in March 1938?

★ d   'News of the *Anschluss* caused considerable popular alarm in Italy, and brought no popularity to the Fascist regime' (Thomson). Consider this quotation in the light of the above 'telephone conversation'.

5   President Roosevelt's Message

The fabric of peace on the continent of Europe, if not throughout the rest of the world, is in immediate danger. The consequences of its rupture are incalculable. Should hostilities break out, the lives of millions of men, women and children in every country involved
5   will most certainly be lost under circumstances of unspeakable horror.

The economic system of every country involved is certain to be shattered. The social structure of every country involved may well be completely wrecked.

10   The supreme desire of the American people is to live in peace. But in the event of a general war they face the fact that no nation can escape some measure of the consequences of such a world catastrophe.

It is my conviction that all people under the threat of war to-
15   day pray that peace may be made before, rather than after, war.

On behalf of the one hundred and thirty millions of people of the United States of America and for the sake of humanity everywhere I most earnestly appeal to you not to break off negotiations, looking to a peaceful, fair and constructive settlement
20   of the questions at issue.

I earnestly repeat that so long as negotiations continue differences may be reconciled. Once they are broken off reason is banished and force asserts itself.

And force produces no solution for the future good of humanity.

Quoted in Sumner Welles, *The Time for Decision*, p 58.

This message was sent to Neville Chamberlain, M. Daladier, President Beneš and Hitler on Monday, 26 September 1938, at 1.00 a.m.

Questions

★ *a* 'The fabric of peace . . . is in immediate danger' (lines 1–2). What steps did President Roosevelt take *before* and *after* 26 September 1938 to prevent the outbreak of war in Europe?

b What impression of the American attitude to Europe do you derive from Roosevelt's message?

c Without making use of the benefit of hindsight, would you call the Munich Agreement 'peaceful, fair and constructive' (line 19)?

6 Sudetenland: Hitler's 'Last Territorial Demand'

(a) Hitler at the Sportspalast, 26 September 1938

This is the last territorial demand I have to make in Europe, but it is a demand on which I will not yield.

Its history is as follows: in 1918 Central Europe was torn up and reshaped by some foolish or crazy so-called statesmen under the
5 slogan 'self-determination and the right of nations'.

Without regard to history, origin of peoples, their national wishes, their economic necessities, they smashed up Europe and arbitrarily set up new States.

To this, Czechoslovakia owed its existence. . . .
10 Mr Wilson's right of self-determination for the 3,500,000 [Sudeten Germans] must be enforced and we shall not just look on any longer. . . .

And now, in fact, England and France agreed to dispatch the only possible demand to Czechoslovakia, namely to free the
15 German region and cede it to the Reich.

I am thankful to Mr. Chamberlain for all his trouble and I assured him that the German people wants nothing but peace . . .

I also assured him and I repeat here that if this problem is solved, there will be no further territorial problems in Europe for
20 Germany. . . . We do not want any Czechs.

Reproduced in Lewis Copeland, op cit, pp 505–6

(b) A diarist's impressions

Monday, 26 September 1938. The news is grave. France, Britain and Czechoslovakia do not accept the Hitler memorandum. Like two meteors travelling through space, the two forces in Europe are now moving on a collision line and the final catastrophe seems
25 inevitable. Trenches are being dug in Hyde Park today; anti-aircraft Territorials were called up. Parliament is to meet on Wednesday.

At eight Hitler addressed a frenzied crowd in the Sportpalast in
Berlin. We listened in to Rupert's little set and heard very clearly.
30 It was a violent speech – delivered in a raucous, ranting voice. His
violent denunciation of Beneš was like the raving of a lunatic.
There was no trace of conciliation in his speech. He did not
entirely bar the door to peace. He gave the Czechs until October
1st to hand over the Sudeten areas which he has fixed in his
35 memorandum. After the 9.40 news Harold Nicolson spoke on the
events of the week. He was bitter and sarcastic about Germany.
Defined the issue as two problems: (1) The Germans wanted their
compatriots in the Sudetenlands; they could have them; (2) they
wanted to destroy the independence of Czechoslovakia; that they
40 could not be allowed to do.

> *The Diaries of Sir Robert Bruce Lockhart*, vol i: 1915–1938,
> ed. Kenneth Young (London, Macmillan, 1973), p 397

Questions

* a In the light of the third paragraph of Hitler's speech (extract *a*),
     illustrate and briefly account for the major differences separating
     the Czechs and Slovaks in their social, economic and cultural
     development.
  b 'What made possible the creation of Czechoslovakia was . . .
     the collapse of Austria-Hungary in 1918' (Anthony Polonsky).
     Examine this statement in an attempt to assess the historical
     validity of Hitler's claim in lines 3–5.
* c Why should Hitler be 'thankful to Mr. Chamberlain' (line 16)?
  d Identify 'the Hitler memorandum' (line 22). Why was it
     unacceptable to France and Britain?
* e 'Without his help it would have been impossible to avoid a
     European war' (Lord Halifax on Beneš). Who is Beneš (line
     31)? What considerations influenced his reaction to Hitler's
     demands? How did he 'help' to 'avoid a European war'?
  f Do you find Harold Nicolson's definition of the Czechoslovak
     issue as it stood on 26 September 1938 historically accurate and
     realistic? Could Hitler's 'last territorial demand' be satisfied
     without in fact destroying 'the independence of Czechoslovakia'
     (line 39)?

7 Treason at Munich?

Germany, the United Kingdom, France, and Italy, taking into
consideration the settlement already agreed upon in principle
concerning the cession of the Sudeten German districts, have
agreed on the following conditions and procedure and the measures
5 to be taken, and declare themselves individually held responsible

by this agreement for guaranteeing the steps necessary for its fulfilment:

1. The evacuation begins on October 1.

2. The United Kingdom of Great Britain, France and Italy agree that the evacuation of the region shall be completed by October 10 . . .

3. The conditions governing the evacuation will be laid down in detail by an international commission composed of representatives of Germany, the United Kingdom, France, Italy, and Czechoslovakia.

4. The occupation by stages of the predominantly Sudeten German territories by German troops will begin on October 1. The four territories marked on the . . . map will be occupied by German troops in the following order:- The territory marked No. 1 on October 1 and 2, the territory marked No. 2 on October 2 and 3, the territory marked No. 3 on October 3, 4, and 5, the territory marked No. 4 on October 6 and 7.

The remaining territories of predominantly German character will be ascertained by the aforesaid international commission forthwith and be occupied by German troops by October 10.

5. The international commission referred to in paragraph 3 will determine the territories in which a plebiscite is to be held. These territories will be occupied by international bodies until the plebiscite has been completed. The same commission will fix the conditions in which the plebiscite is to be held, taking as a basis the conditions of the Saar plebiscite. . . .

6. The final determination of the frontier will be carried out by the international commission. . . .

7. There will be a right of option into and out of the transferred territories, the option to be exercised within six months of the date of this agreement. . . .

8. The Czechoslovak Government will within the period of four weeks from the date of this agreement release from the military and police forces any Sudeten Germans who may wish to be released, and the Czechoslovak Government will within the same period release Sudeten German prisoners who are serving terms of imprisonment for political offences.

The Munich Agreement, 29 September 1938. Reproduced in S. Grant Duff, *Europe and the Czechs* (Harmondsworth, Penguin Special, revised edition, October 1938), pp 246–7

Questions

a   Identify and comment briefly on (i) 'the settlement already agreed upon in principle' (line 2); (ii) 'the conditions of the Saar plebiscite' (line 31).

★   b   Why was Czechoslovakia not represented at Munich?

★   c   Explain the main differences between the Munich Agreement and Hitler's Godesberg Memorandum which had been rejected by both France and Britain. What historical significance do these differences have?

d 'What was meant as appeasement had turned into capitulation' (A. J. P. Taylor). Do you agree with this assessment of the Munich Agreement?

8 Chamberlain's Appeasement Policy

(a) Chamberlain defends Munich Agreement, House of Commons, 3 October 1938

Hard things have been said about the German Chancellor today and in the past, but I do feel that the House ought to recognize the difficulty for a man in that position to take back such an emphatic declaration as he had already made and to recognize that in
5 consenting, even though it were only at the last minute, to discuss with the representatives of the other powers those things which he had declared he had already decided once and for all, was a real contribution on his part.

As regards Signor Mussolini, his contribution was certainly
10 notable, and perhaps decisive. It was on his suggestion that the final stages of mobilisation were postponed for twenty-four hours, to give us an opportunity of discussing the situation, and I wish to say that at the conference itself both he and the Italian Foreign Secretary, Count Ciano, were most helpful in the discussion.
15 It was they who, very early in the proceeding, produced a memorandum which Daladier and I were able to accept as a basis of discussion.

I think Europe and the world have reason to be grateful to the head of the Italian government for contributing to a peaceful
20 solution. . . . The question of Czechoslovakia is the latest and perhaps the most dangerous. Now that we have got past it I feel that it may be possible to make further progress along the road to sanity. . . .

I am too much of a realist to believe that we are going to
25 achieve our purpose in a day. We have only laid the foundations of peace. The superstructure is not even begun.

Reproduced in Lewis Copeland, op cit, pp 457–9

(b) A dissentient Conservative's disapproval

And I will say this, that I believe the Czechs, left to themselves, and told they were going to get no help from the Western Powers, would have been able to make better terms than they have got
30 after all this tremendous perturbation. They could hardly have done worse.

All is over. Silent, mournful, abandoned, broken, Czechoslovakia
recedes into the darkness. She has suffered in every respect by her
associations with France, under whose guidance and policy she has
35 been actuated for so long.
        Winston S. Churchill, op cit, p 256

(c) A historian's view

We may now stand back and look at the record of Chamberlain's
appeasement policy. Appeasement of Italy, so far as it was
practised, justified itself to the hilt; the appalling tragedy is that
this policy was not worked out to the full as Chamberlain wished
40 it. Appeasement of Germany is much more vulnerable to criticism,
but not from the angle from which that criticism is usually
launched. A policy of backing up French bluff over Czechoslovakia
would almost certainly have resulted in that bluff being called.
Perhaps Germany would have fought a very brief war against the
45 Czechs; almost certainly both France and Russia would have
avoided taking effective action in the matter. Thus would clear
notice have been served on all the smaller European nations that
resistance to Germany was futile.
    There remains a possible criticism of appeasement from the
50 opposite angle: that Britain was wrong to press her mediation on
the Czechs; that she should have kept out of any involvement
with countries which she was not in a position to assist directly in
event of trouble. This is a much more powerful criticism of
Chamberlain's policy, but it is not one which is often advanced.
        Roy Douglas, 'Chamberlain and Appeasement', in *The*
        Fascist Challenge and the Policy of Appeasement, eds Wolfgang
        J. Mommmsen and Lothar Kettenacker (London, George
        Allen & Unwin, 1983), pp 87–8

Questions

a   Identify and comment on (i) 'such an emphatic declaration'
    (lines 3–4); (ii) 'a memorandum' (lines 15–16); (iii) 'her
    associations with France' (lines 33–4).
b   'We have only laid the foundations of peace' (lines 25–6).
    Consider Chamberlain's attitude to 'the German Chancellor' in
    the first paragraph of extract *a* in the light of David Thomson's
    claim that '[t]he policy of appeasement had failed because it
    was based upon a fundamental misconception of the nature of
    National Socialism and of Hitler himself'.
c   In what ways was Mussolini's 'contribution' (line 8) to the
    final settlement of the Munich Agreement 'certainly notable,
    and perhaps decisive' (lines 9–10)?
d   'Thou art weighed in the balance and found wanting'. In the

light of extract *c*, is this a fair judgement on the performance of
the western democracies at Munich?

   e Do you find Churchill's 'disapproval' in extract *b* convincing?

★ *f* Do you agree with Anthony Adamthwaite that 'France could
and should have fought in 1938'?

★ *g* Is it historically justified to claim that the Munich Agreement
'deranged' the 'whole equilibrium of Europe'?

★ *h* How far do you consider appeasement a true cause of the
Second World War?

9 The Munich Conference and Public Opinion

(a) 'The Times', Saturday, 1 October 1938

No conqueror returning from a victory on the battlefield has
come home adorned with nobler laurels than Mr. Chamberlain
from Munich yesterday; and the King and people alike have
shown by the manner of their reception their sense of his
5 achievement. . . .

    Had the Government of the United Kingdom been in less
resolute hands, it is as certain as it can be that war, incalculable in
its range, would have broken out against the wishes of every
people concerned. The horror of such a catastrophe was not least
10 in Germany. So much is clear from the immense popular
enthusiasm with which Mr. Chamberlain was greeted on each of
his three visits; a crowd of that disciplined nation does not break
through a police cordon to acclaim a foreign statesman out of
conventional politeness. Indeed, these visits seem to have increased
15 the Fuehrer's understanding of his own people's sentiments, with
a definite effect upon his policy.

    Let us hope that he may go on to see the wisdom of allowing
them at all times to know the sentiments of other peoples instead
of imposing between them a smoke-screen of ignorance and
20 propaganda. For our own nation it remains to show our gratitude
to Mr. Chamberlain, chiefly by learning the lessons taught by the
great dangers through which we have been so finely led – that
only a people prepared to face the worst can, through their
leaders, cause peace to prevail in a crisis; but that the threat of ruin
25 to civilisation will recur unless injustices are faced and removed in
quiet times, instead of being left to fester until it is too late for
remedy.

(b) 'Evening Standard', Friday, 30 September 1938

Criticism will be directed against the British and French
Governments for failing to secure better terms. The unanswerable

30   argument in their favour is that this agreement is better than the
irreparable catastrophe of war. Even so, M. Daladier's political
position in France may be difficult. His reply to critics must be
that the lesson for France is that she needs greatly to strengthen
her air force and her preparedness. From Britain's standpoint there
35   is only one feature in the agreement which will cause regret – the
guarantee of Czechoslovakia's revised frontiers to which we are
committed.

(c) 'The Star', Friday, 30 September 1938

The bill has still to be sent in and met. The matters which have
now been settled without war and are to be the subject of
40   consultation instead of war between this country and Germany
have led to the expenditure of millions of armaments. The recent
weeks of crisis in this country have involved an expenditure of
public and private funds of which we shall never have an
accounting. We may well be grateful for the outcome, but we are
45   entitled to resent the expensive and unreasonable process.

      All these extracts are reproduced in W. W. Hadley, *Munich:
Before and After* (London, Cassell, 1944), pp 94, 97, 98

Questions

a   Explain briefly the purpose of 'each of [Chamberlain's] three
visits' (lines 11–12) to Germany.
b   What evidence is there to support *The Times*' claim that 'the
immense popular enthusiasm' (lines 10–11) which greeted
Chamberlain in Germany had 'a definite effect' (line 15) upon
Hitler's policy?
c   Identify 'the guarantee' (lines 35–6) and suggest reasons why it
should 'cause regret' (line 35) eventually.
d   'The bill has still to be sent in and met' (line 38). Explain and
comment briefly on *The Star*'s criticism in extract *c*.
e   What lessons, according to the three extracts, can be learned
from the Munich crisis? What other lessons would you draw
from this experience?
f   What value would you give to contemporary press criticism as
historical evidence?

10   The Case of France

The three years from 1936 to 1939 began and ended in broken
promises. In July 1936 Blum promised help to the sister Spanish
Republic but within a few weeks initiated the policy of
non-intervention. In September 1938 notwithstanding several

5   reassertions of alliance obligations, Daladier, on his own admission,
     was 'like a barbarian' ready 'to cut up' Czechoslovakia 'without
     even consulting her'. In September 1939 although France fulfilled
     the letter of her Polish alliance nothing was done to honour its
     spirit. Poland was overrun in a matter of weeks while from the
10   Maginot line French troops watched the Germans playing football.
        The principal aim of French foreign policy was the search for an
     agreement with Germany. French Prime Ministers from Blum to
     Daladier worked consistently for an understanding with Hitler.
     But the price of Franco-German amity was the liquidation of
15   French interests in central and eastern Europe. No French
     government was prepared to pay such a price. Even Bonnet
     fought shy of denouncing France's eastern pacts. Nevertheless
     French Ministers were ready to go a long way towards meeting
     Germany's expansionist aims. Hand in hand with advances to
20   Berlin went a gradual disengagement from the east.
        After Munich, the search for agreement with the dictators went
     into top gear. Despite the acrimony which had soured relations
     between the Latin sisters since the Ethiopian crisis, the Daladier
     ministry strove hard to reach a settlement. Only Italian perversity
25   prevented an agreement in the autumn of 1938. Approaches to
     Germany were more successful. With a Franco-German declaration
     of 6 December 1938, France achieved a counterpart to the Anglo-
     German declaration of 30 September 1938. Contrary to what was
     said at the time and afterwards, Germany was not given a free
30   hand in the east. However, reading between the lines it is clear
     that the French government was willing to tolerate German
     expansion in the east, provided it was peaceful and kept within
     bounds.
        In the winter of 1938–39 the retreat from eastern Europe
35   continued apace. For all practical purposes, the Czech alliance was
     dissolved and Ministers showed little interest in securing for
     Prague the international guarantee promised in the Munich
     agreement. The Franco-Soviet pact was said to have died a natural
     death and the Soviet government was kept at arm's length. Bonnet
40   and his Ambassador at Warsaw, Léon Noel, also talked of revising
     the Franco-Polish alliance of 1921. Criticism of the government's
     foreign policy was not strong enough to deflect Daladier and
     Bonnet from their central purpose. . . .
        Hitler's annexation of Bohemia and Moravia on 15 March 1939
45   led to a diplomatic revolution. Britain and France gave guarantees
     to Poland, Greece and Rumania. Negotiations were initiated for
     alliances with the Soviet Union and Turkey. Under Daladier's
     direction, French diplomacy after 15 March was much firmer than
     at any time since Poincaré's premiership in the early 1920s.
50   Unfortunately, British and French policy was not firm enough to
     convince Hitler that a European war would follow an attack on

Poland. . . . The hastily cobbled 'peace front' of March–April, for which Soviet participation was belatedly sought, was essentially a diplomatic combination designed to corral Hitler into new negotiations.

> Anthony Adamthwaite, *France and the Coming of the Second World War 1936–1939* (London, Frank Cass, 1977), pp 353–54

Questions

    a Identify (i) Blum (line 2); (ii) Daladier (line 5); (iii) 'the Maginot line' (lines 9–10); (iv) Bonnet (line 16); (v) 'the Latin sisters' (line 23); (vi) Poincaré (line 49).

★ *b* What were the 'French interests in central and eastern Europe' (line 15)? How did these considerations influence France's relations with Germany during this period?

★ *c* Briefly account for France's 'broken promises' (lines 1–2) between 1936 and 1939.

★ *d* 'Hand in hand with advances to Berlin went a gradual disengagement from the east' (lines 19–20). In the light of this statement, consider Adamthwaite's other view that 'For France, Munich was a bloodless Sedan, completing the decline which the Rhineland coup had begun in March 1936'.

    e Explain the historical significance of (i) 'Franco-German declaration of 6 December 1938' (lines 26–7); (ii) 'Anglo-German declaration of 30 September 1938' (lines 27–8); (iii) 'the Czech alliance' (line 35); (iv) 'The Franco-Soviet pact' (line 38).

★ *f* Assess the historical accuracy of the term 'a diplomatic revolution' in line 45.

VIII   War breaks out in Europe

Introduction

Hitler's occupation of Bohemia and Moravia – 'the real Czechoslovakia' – on 15 March 1939 woke the appeasers to the bitter reality of the situation. The *Wehrmacht*'s advance into Prague, in cynical violation of the Munich Agreement, 'unmasked' and 'discredited' the true Adolf Hitler. Those who for long had sought a *modus vivendi* with Hitler's political philosophy and had been placidly acquiescing in his arbitrary remoulding of the map of Europe suddenly woke up to realise that 'the Nazi aims' were no longer compatible 'with any conception of their own national interests' (Lord Beloff). Hitler's 'act of piracy on the Ides of March' discredited with equal force *their* policy of appeasement to which the *Führer* 'had owed much of his success' (Kochan). In his *Failure of a Mission* Neville Henderson, re-echoing his master's voice, claims that 'it is no exaggeration to say that in 1939 . . . the war has been caused by the deliberate tearing up of a scrap of paper.' Rather, I incline to the view that it was Britain and France who had allowed, and at times even encouraged, Hitler's defiance of sacred international treaties.

'Prague,' says Henderson, 'revitalised France, consolidated England and the Empire and produced a common front against future German aggression.' This raises the somewhat controversial question whether Prague did in fact bring appeasement to an end, or whether, as Soviet historians claim, 'the old policy' was henceforth 'conducted by other means' (Margot Light). Was not Hitler after all 'allowed' to annex the city of Memel barely a week after the liquidation of Czechoslovakia? Such an attitude was confirmed in the summer of 1939 by the western democracies' reluctance to pursue seriously their negotiations with the Soviet Union to withstand in a common front Hitler's blatant ambitions. Instead of turning 'Nazi Germany onto the Soviet Union, in the hope that Fascism and Socialism would mutually annihilate one another' (Light), their dilatory manner was in part responsible for the Nazi–Soviet Pact of 23 August 1939. Whatever cultural prejudices mould western historians' scepticism, the Soviets had reason to nourish profound suspicions of the sincerity of the western powers.

Fascist Italy too became conscious of the real situation. Italy, which had ostensibly conveyed through the years the image of a warlike Great Power – Albania, perhaps in emulation of Prague, was Mussolini's 'last splutter of indignation' (Taylor) – found herself unprepared when the outbreak of war looked imminent. The image was in the first place deceptive both to the Italians themselves and to the rest of the world. Secondly, the Spanish Civil War had drained the Fascist State of its energy and its resources. It was perhaps this act of self-awareness, imposed by the rapidly deteriorating circumstances, which in part explains Count Ciano's 'disgust' with Nazi Germany in August 1939, his idea of summoning a conference – similar to that of Munich – to consider the future of Poland, and, only a few months after the Pact of Steel had been signed, the humiliating posture of neutrality which naked realism, divested of all self-deluding party propaganda, forced the *Duce* and his Italy to adopt.

Basically, Hitler's 'outrageous' demands, which he presented to Poland shortly after Prague 'in the form of a direct threat', consisted in the return to the Reich of the free city of Danzig (Gdánsk) and the so-called Polish Corridor for 'the rail and road connections with East Prussia across Pomerania' (Józef Garliński). To the united Poles these conditions were synonymous with 'the destruction of Polish independence'. On 31 March 1939 Britain guaranteed full military support for Poland in the event of German aggression, and extended it to Greece and Roumania after Mussolini's attack on Albania. This military guarantee was subsequently replaced by an Anglo–Polish alliance, two days after the Rippentrop–Molotov Pact. It was 'linked with the strengthening of [Poland's] alliance with France' (O. Halecki). 'The British guarantee to Poland,' says A. J. P. Taylor, 'led directly to the outbreak of war in Europe. Hitler, far from being deterred, was provoked.' But there were other, perhaps more important, factors which determined the course of events. To what extent, for example, did the highly critical economic situation in Germany in 1939 (William Carr) influence Hitler's final decision? How far was Hitler's concern 'about the deteriorating balance' of Germany's 'military power' (*idem*) a fundamental reason for his invasion of Poland? How far was Hitler's conviction that France and Britain would ultimately lack 'the will to fight' for Poland a decisive factor'?

'Hitler's war' was launched by a Nazi *Blitzkrieg* on Poland in the small hours of 1 September 1939. After a 'wilful' delay of two days Britain declared war on Germany. 'The Chamberlain government, in order to remain in power, bowed to the will of Parliament and probably of the country' (Taylor). In the afternoon of the same day Daladier, who 'for the last five years . . . had been following events without the power to control them'

(Cobban) did likewise. Both allies were unprepared. Both had practically 'to restrict themselves to military activities that were hardly more than spectacular demonstrations' (Halecki).

1   The Exploitation of Bohemia

(a) The 'Nationalzeitung' of Basle, a leading Swiss paper, reports on 7 June 1939

From the industrial parts all observers report a systematic exploitation of the country in favour of Germany. Three months ago there was all over the country a superfluity of foodstuffs and luxury articles, of clothes, fabrics, and all articles of everyday
5   requirement, and the price level was far below that ruling in neighbouring Germany. To-day you cannot even get the essentials of life. Czechoslovakia's great supplies of grain have been carried off to Germany. A country has been hurled from a state of prosperity and content into destitution and want, without the
10 majority of the Germans in the Reich benefiting in the slightest from the fruits of this plundering expedition.
> Reproduced in Eugene Lennhoff, op cit, p 73

(b) A historian's comment

Hitler was right in supposing that the western democracies would, as usual, only protest at the rape of Czechoslovakia. What he did not anticipate was the deep impression the events of March 1939
15 made upon public opinion in Britain. Overnight, appeasement was discredited; Hitler had not acted in a civilised fashion, as Chamberlain had hoped; on the contrary he had deliberately plotted to destroy Czechoslovakia. Nor could Hitler claim to be reuniting Germans any more; Czechs and Slovaks were not
20 German by any stretch of the imagination. At last it dawned on public opinion that Hitler was seeking to dominate Europe by force. Although Chamberlain did not completely abandon the appeasement policy, he began to pay more attention to rearmament and at long last tried to create a diplomatic front in Europe capable
25 of containing the Germans.
> William Carr, A History of Germany 1815–1945 (London, Edward Arnold, 1969), p 408

(c) The Good Czechs' Ten Commandments

1. Believe in the right of the eight million Czechs to live in an independent state.
2. Believe in the justice of history, which will not long tolerate the oppression of this sacred right.

30 3. Do not believe that we have lived for a thousand years within the German Reich. History shows that this is false.

4. Do not believe what the Czech newspapers and wireless tell you. They tell you what the Germans make the editors and announcers say.

35 5. Do not believe that our political leaders agree to the joining of our country to Germany. They have to be careful and pretend to be loyal, otherwise there would be no more Czechs left in responsible positions.

6. Do not believe that we have been abandoned. Beneš is working

40 zealously. He has thousands of friends and helpers, both Czechs and foreigners, who are not silent even here in their own country, as you can see every day.

7. You must not only speak, but think as Czechs.

8. Behave properly, but coldly to the Germans, so that they feel

45 that they are strangers here, and in the service of injustice and force.

9. Do not attend German festivities and military parades. That is treason and good propaganda for the German cinema.

10. Never forget that the German army has seized a booty of 40

50 milliard crowns, which our beloved republic collected by the sweat of Czech brows. Never forget September 1938 and our humiliation on 15 March 1939. Be strong and stir up the weak! Believe in Beneš! Believe in our national motto: '*Pravda Vitezi*' ('Truth Prevails').

> A pamphlet, secretly circulated in 'millions of copies'. Reproduced in Eugene Lennhoff, op cit, pp 75–6

Questions

★ a 'To-day you cannot even get the essentials of life' (lines 6–7). Account briefly for what happened 'Three months ago' (lines 2–3) to cause so much change in Bohemia.

b '[A]ll observers report' (line 1). How far are eye-witnesses' reports reliable as historical evidence?

c '[T]he execution of the Munich agreement [far] exceeded even the concessions agreed to' (Thomson). In the light of this quotation, consider briefly what Hitler gained by 'this plundering expedition' (line 11).

d What did 'the western democracies' (line 12) lose?

e How can 'public opinion' (lines 15, 21) in Britain or elsewhere be gauged?

★ f What impression of Hitler do you get from extracts a and b? What further attempts did Chamberlain make after March 1939 to appease Hitler?

g What does extract c reveal about 'the rape of Czechoslovakia' (line 13)?

h What insight does this 'pamphlet' (extract *c*) provide into 'the psychology and method' of the Czech national resistance movement?

2 Danzig: 'Not a Place but a Principle'

One of the Secretaries at the German Embassy, Herr von Selzem, had been a good friend of mine in Calcutta, and we had seen quite a lot of him and his American wife in London. One day he asked me to lunch to meet a member of the faculty of the Technische
5   Hochschule at Danzig. The Professor spoke perfect English, and we had scarcely sat down before he embarked upon a long rigmarole about the Danzig situation. When he had finished, I told him that I was already familiar with the problem, and that it seemed to me that there was plenty of room for patient discussion.
10   On the other hand, the use or even the threat of violence would achieve nothing, and might lead to terrible consequences. 'But surely England would not fight for Danzig?' he asked. I replied that this was a matter for the Government, but that personally I devoutly hoped that we would. Carton de Wiart, who was living
15   in Poland, had just written to me to say that Danzig was 'no longer a place but a principle', and I used these words to describe how public opinion in England regarded the matter. I expected this to enrage the professor, but he merely looked patronising. 'What could you do to save Poland?' he asked. This was exactly
20   what I had been waiting for. I readily acknowledged that we could probably do very little to prevent Poland from being overrun in the first instance, any more than we had been able to prevent Belgium from being overrun in 1914. But we had hoped then, and we hoped now, that the knowledge that Great Britain would go
25   to war if the integrity of countries to whom we had given a guarantee was violated, would restrain any aggressor. The Germany of Kaiser Wilhelm II had disregarded the warning and had paid the penalty. Surely Hitler's Germany would not repeat the mistake! By this time I was worked up and forgot my
30   manners. 'Let there be no mistake about it, Professor. If you force us to go to war, we will get you in the end, as we got you last time.' After that there was not much more to be said. The party broke up.

    The Memoirs of General the Lord Ismay (London, William Heinemann, 1960), pp 95–6

Questions

a Identify and comment on 'the problem' of Danzig referred to in line 8. What does, do you think, the author mean by 'there was plenty of room for patient discussion' (line 9)?

b What do you understand by 'no longer a place but a principle' (lines 15–16)? Considering Britain's past performance, how much credibility would you give to this claim?

★ *c* To what extent and in what ways was public opinion in Britain a determining factor in foreign policy during the interwar period?

★ *d* What did public opinion expect Britain to do 'to save Poland' (line 19)?

★ *e* How would you assess the value of memoirs such as Lord Ismay's as historical evidence?

3 The Conquest of Albania

Italian Embassy, London
April 7th, XVII (1939).

Duce,

Today's events have 'electrified' my spirits. Our troops in
5 Valona! In a few hours *the whole* of Albania will be ours, it will be
a '*Province*' of the Empire! After the vengeance for Adowa, the
vengeance for Valona. You, Duce, are making the Revolution
move with the inevitable and ruthless motion of a tractor whose
tracks take hold, crush, and relinquish hold only when the next
10 track has already begun to crush.

I remember having once read, whether in Tacitus or Suetonius I
don't know, that Augustus would not celebrate the victory of the
Empire until the day Tiberius sent him the news that Illyria, the
bastion of Rome, had been definitively conquered.

15 The Roman Empire was born of two wars: Scipio's war in
Spain, and Caesar's war in Albania. Today it is Caesar's legions –
your legions – who are crossing the sea again, at exactly the same
spot, for the first time for two thousand years.

Your faithful collaborator who for eight years has had the
20 privilege of being a daily witness of your work in Albania, knows
that you have never relaxed your efforts, even for a moment, that
your marching-orders were *one alone* and that one alone was the
definitive solution for which you were preparing, *the definitive and
permanent military conquest of Albania.*

25 This conquest makes the Adriatic a strategically Italian sea *for the
first time*, and opens the ancient highways of Roman conquest in
the East to Mussolini's Italy.

But the conquest of Albania means not only security in the
Adriatic; the pincer which immobilises Belgrade for good; and the
30 starting-point for a march through the Balkans and the East. It is
much more; it automatically means a fresh military defeat for
England in the Mediterranean, because it puts Greece at our
mercy; Greece, which the English Admiralty has hitherto

considered the natural and indispensable stronghold of England in
35 her naval war in the Mediterranean.

You once said in the Grand Council that one of the *decisive*
reasons for our African victory was our having *forced* the English,
through sending the two motorised divisions to Cyrenaica, to *land
warfare*. And that, Duce, was one of your profoundest truths.
40 Your two divisions in Cyrenaica, on the Egyptian frontier, were
the key to your strategic plan and the preliminary to victory in
Africa.

Your legions in Albania – which means, wherever you wish in
Greece – denote another 'land war' which you have imposed on
45 the English, with the latter's automatic loss of the two naval bases
and our complete domination of the Eastern Mediterranean.

[Dino] GRANDI.

Reproduced, with italics, in *Benito Mussolini: Memoirs 1942–
43, With Documents relating to the period*, ed. Raymond
Klibansky, trans. Frances Lobb (London, George Weidenfeld
& Nicolson, 1949), pp 199–200

Questions

a Identify (i) 'Today's events' (line 4); (ii) 'your work in Albania'
   (line 20).
b Explain the historical context of Dino Grandi's remark 'After
   the vengeance for Adowa, the vengeance for Valona' (lines 6–
   7).
c Comment briefly on the effectiveness of the 'tractor' image in
   lines 7–10.
★ d What considerations do you think influenced Mussolini's
      decision to conquer Albania in April 1939?
e Assess the historical validity of Grandi's claim concerning 'the
   key' to Mussolini's 'victory in Africa' in lines 36–42.
★ f Consider briefly the international repercussions of Mussolini's
      conquest of Albania.
g What does Grandi's letter reveal of (i) his state of mind; (ii) the
   nature of Fascism?

4   An Assessment of Poland's Predicament

(a) Count Ciano's view

16 April [1939]. Two long conversations with Goering . . . I was
most struck by the tone in which he described relations with
Poland. It was strangely reminiscent of the tone which not so long
ago was used in Germany with regard to Austria and
5 Czechoslovakia. Yet the Germans are mistaken if they think that
they can carry on in the same manner. The Poles will be beaten;

but they will not lay down their arms without a fierce and bloody struggle.

17 April [1939]. I accompanied Goering to the station. On the whole, I got the impression that peaceful intentions still prevail even in Germany. Poland is the only danger that exists. I was less impressed by the substance of the comments directed against Warsaw, than by their contemptuous tone. The Germans should not imagine that they are simply going to hold a victory parade in Poland. If the Poles are attacked, they will fight. The Duce is of the same opinion.

15 May [1939]. Conversation with Wieniawa [the retiring Polish Ambassador in Rome] . . . I urged him to show the greatest moderation. Whatever will happen, Poland will pay the cost of the conflict. No Franco–British assistance will be forthcoming, at least, not in the first phase of the war; and Poland would quickly be turned into a heap of ruins. Wieniawa admits that I am right on many points, but believes in some eventual success that might give Poland greater strength. Alas, I fear that many, too many, Poles share his illusions.

> *Ciano's Diaries, 1939–43*, ed. Malcolm Muggeridge (London, 1947). Reproduced in Norman Davies, *God's Playground: A History of Poland* (Oxford, Clarendon Press, 1981), vol ii, p 432

(b) Hitler's view, 23 May 1939

Further successes can no longer be attained without the shedding of blood. . . .

Danzig is not the object of our activities. It is a question of expanding our living-space in the east, of securing our food-supplies, and of settling the Baltic problem. . . . There is no question of sparing Poland and we are left with the decision: To attack Poland at the first suitable opportunity.

We cannot expect a repetition of the Czech affair. There will be war. Our task is to isolate Poland. The success of this isolation will be decisive. . . . There must be no simultaneous conflict with the Western Powers.

If it is not certain that German–Polish conflict will not lead to war in the west, the fight must be primarily against England and France.

Basic principle: Conflict with Poland – beginning with an attack on Poland – will only be successful if the Western Powers keep out. If this is impossible, then it will be better to attack in the west and incidentally to settle Poland at the same time.

> Reproduced in Alan Bullock, op cit, pp 509–10

Questions

a What do you think Ciano intended to suggest by his remarks on Goering's 'tone' in the first two paragraphs of extract a?

b What impression of Ciano's personal views on Poland do you derive from extract a? How far do they conform with Mussolini's?

c What 'eventual success' (line 23), do you think, could have possibly given Poland 'greater strength' (line 24)? Is it justified to call the Poles' belief in such an 'eventual success' illusive?

d What, according to extract b, does Hitler mean by 'a repetition of the Czech affair' (line 33)?

★ e 'There is no question of sparing Poland' (lines 30–1). What were Hitler's demands on Poland? Why were these rejected by the Polish government?

5 Ciano Disgusted with Nazi Germany

(a) After the Salzburg experience, 13 August 1939

I returned to Rome [from Salzburg] completely disgusted with the Germans, with their leader, with their way of doing things. They have betrayed us and lied to us. Now they are dragging us into an adventure which we have not wanted and which might compromise
5 the régime and the country as a whole. The Italian people will boil over with horror when they know about the aggression against Poland and most probably will wish to fight the Germans. I don't know whether to wish Italy a victory or Germany a defeat. In any case, given the German attitude, I think that our hands are free,
10 and I propose that we act accordingly, declaring that we have no intention of participating in a war which we have neither wanted nor provoked.

The Duce's reactions are varied. At first he agrees with me. Then he says the honour compels him to march with Germany.
15 Finally, he states that he wants his part of the booty in Croatia and Dalmatia.

(b) Ciano to Mussolini, 21 August 1939

You cannot and you must not do it. The faithfulness with which I served you in the politics of the Axis authorises me to speak clearly. I went to Salzburg to arrange a common line of agreement.
20 I found myself faced with a German diktat. The Germans – not us – have betrayed the alliance in which we were associates not servants. Rip up the pact, throw it in Hitler's face and Europe will recognise you as the natural leader of the anti-German crusade.

Do you want me to go to Salzburg [again]? Alright I'll go and I'll
25 speak to the Germans as is necessary.

> Both excerpts from *Ciano's Diaries*, as reproduced in C. J.
> Lowe and F. Marzari, op cit, pp 412, 342

Questions

a   What was Ciano's mission to Salzburg?
b   Suggest reasons why Ciano felt 'disgusted' (line 1) by his
    Salzburg experience. What evidence is there to support his
    claim that the Germans 'have betrayed us and lied to us' (line
    3)?
c   Identify (i) 'the politics of the Axis' (line 18); (ii) 'the pact' (line
    22).
d   How would you explain Ciano's concern for the reaction of
    'The Italian people' in lines 5–7?
★ e 'You cannot and you must not do it' (line 17). How far did
    Ciano's 'outburst' influence Mussolini's reappraisal of Italy's
    posture vis-à-vis Germany?

6   Hitler's Speech to the Commanders-in-Chief, 22 August 1939

I have called you together to give you a picture of the political
situation, in order that you may have some insight into the
individual factors on which I have based my decision to act and in
order to strengthen your confidence. . . .
5   First of all, two personal factors: my own personality and that
of Mussolini. Essentially all depends on me, on my existence,
because of my political talents. Probably no one will ever again
have the confidence of the whole German people as I have. There
will probably never again be a man with more authority than I
10 have. My existence is therefore a factor of great value. But I can
be eliminated at any time by a criminal or a lunatic. The second
personal factor is the Duce. His existence is also a decisive factor.
If anything happens to him, Italy's loyalty to the alliance will no
longer be certain. . . . The Duce is the man with the strongest
15 nerves in Italy. The third personal factor in our favour is Franco.
We can ask only for benevolent neutrality from Spain. . . . He
guarantees a certain uniformity and stability in the present system
in Spain. . . .
    It is easy for us to make decisions. We have nothing to lose; we
20 have everything to gain. . . . [O]ur economic situation is such that
we cannot hold out more than a few more years. . . . We have no
other choice, we must act. Our opponents will be risking a great
deal and can gain only a little. Britain's stake in a war is

inconceivably great. Our enemies have leaders who are below the
25 average. No personalities. No masters, no men of action. . . .
    The relationship with Poland has become unbearable. . . . My
    proposals to Poland were frustrated by England's intervention.
    Poland changed her tone toward us. A permanent state of tension
    is intolerable. The power of initiative cannot be allowed to pass to
30 others. . . . The probability is still great that the West will not
    intervene. We must take the risk with ruthless determination. . . .
    [S]pecial reasons fortify me in my view. England and France have
    undertaken obligations which neither is in a position to fulfil.
    There is no real rearmament in England, but only propaganda.
35 . . . France is short of men. Little has been done for rearmament.
    The artillery is obsolete. . . . The West has only two possibilities
    for fighting against us: 1. Blockade: it will not be effective because
    of our autarky and because we have sources of supply in Eastern
    Europe. 2. Attack in the West from the Maginot line: I consider
40 this impossible.
    Another possibility would be the violation of Dutch, Belgian,
    and Swiss neutrality. . . . England and France will not violate the
    neutrality of these countries. . . . The enemy had another hope,
    that Russia would become our enemy after the conquest of
45 Poland. The enemy did not reckon with my great strength of
    purpose. Our enemies are small fry. I saw them in Munich. I was
    convinced that Stalin would never accept the English offer.
    Documents of German Foreign Policy, Series D 1936/7–40
    (Washington, D.C., 1956), vol vii, pp 200–204

Questions

a   What criticism would you make of each of 'the individual
    factors' (lines 2–3) which, according to Hitler in this extract, had
    encouraged him 'to act'?
b   Explain and comment briefly on (i) 'England's intervention'
    (line 27); (ii) 'Poland changed her tone toward us' (line 28);
    (iii) 'Stalin would never accept the English offer' (line 47).
c   Assess the historical validity of Hitler's remarks on Britain and
    France in lines 32–40. What other sources would you consult
    to support your arguments?
d   What does Hitler's speech add to your knowledge of 'the
    political situation' in Europe on 22 August 1939?

7   The Nazi–Soviet Pact

(a) *The Secret Protocol: Poland's death warrant*

Moscow, 23 August 1939
On the occasion of the Non-Aggression Pact between the

German Reich and the USSR, the undersigned plenipotentiaries
. . . discussed the boundaries of their respective spheres of influence
5   in Eastern Europe. These conversations led to the following
conclusions: . . .

2. In the event of a territorial and political rearrangement of the
areas belonging to the Polish state the spheres of influence of
Germany and the USSR shall be bounded approximately by the
10   line of the rivers Narew, Vistula, and San.

The question of whether the interests of both parties make
desirable the maintenance of an independent Polish State, and how
such a state should be bounded can only be definitely determined
in the course of further political development.

15   In any event, both Governments will resolve this question by
means of a friendly agreement. . . .

4. This protocol shall be treated by both parties as strictly
secret.

For the Govt. of the   Plenipotentiary of the
20   German Reich   Govt. of the USSR
V. Ribbentrop   V. Molotov

Excerpt reproduced in Norman Davies, op cit, p 433

(b) A historian's view

The public [Nazi–Soviet] Pact . . . provided for mutual non-
aggression. A secret protocol excluded Germany from the Baltic
states and from the eastern parts of Poland. . . . This was, after
25   all, what the Russians had sought to obtain from the Western
Powers. The Nazi–Soviet pact was only another way of doing it
. . . The settlement of Brest–Litovsk was at last undone, with the
consent of Germany, instead of with the backing of the Western
Powers. It was no doubt disgraceful that Soviet Russia should
30   make any agreement with the leading Fascist state; but this
reproach came ill from the statesmen who went to Munich and
who were then sustained in their own countries by great majorities.
The Russians, in fact, did only what the Western statesmen had
hoped to do; and Western bitterness was the bitterness of
35   disappointment. . . .

The pact was neither an alliance nor an agreement for the
partition of Poland. Munich had been a true alliance for partition:
the British and French dictated partition to the Czechs. The Soviet
government undertook no such action against the Poles. They
40   merely promised to remain neutral, which is what the Poles had
always asked them to do and which Western policy implied also.
More than this, the agreement was in the last resort anti-German:
it limited the German advance eastwards in case of war. . . . Both
Hitler and Stalin imagined that they had prevented war, not
45   brought it on. Hitler thought that he would score another Munich

over Poland; Stalin that he had at any rate escaped an unequal war in the present, and perhaps even avoided it altogether.

A. J. P. Taylor, *The Origins* . . ., pp 252–3

Questions

a Identify 'the Non-Aggression Pact' in line 2.

★ b How did this pact undo 'the settlement of Brest–Litovsk' (line 27)?

c 'It was no doubt disgraceful' (line 29). In what sense was the pact an ideological volte-face for Soviet Russia?

d What considerations, in your opinion, encouraged Hitler and his National Socialist movement, 'the bulwark against the danger of Communism' (Halecki), to conclude a Non-Aggression pact with the Soviet Union?

★ e '[T]he bitterness of disappointment' (lines 34–5). Why did the Anglo–French–Russian negotiations of March–August 1939 break down and those between Russia and Germany succeed?

f Assess the validity of A. J. P. Taylor's comments in the last paragraph of extract *b* in the light of the Secret Protocol in extract *a*.

8 Daladier's Personal Appeal to Hitler

(a) Daladier, 26 August 1939

I owe it to you, I owe it to our two peoples to say that the fate of peace still rests solely in your hands. There is nothing to-day which need prevent any longer the pacific solution of the international crisis with honour and dignity for all peoples if the
5 will for peace exists equally on all sides. I can personally guarantee the readiness which Poland has always shown to have recourse to methods of free conciliation. There is not one of the grievances involved by Germany against Poland which might not be submitted to decision by such methods.

(b) Hitler's reply, 27 August 1939

10 Things have gone too far. I do not see the possibility of bringing to a pacific solution a Poland who now feels herself inviolable under the protection of her guarantees . . . or of obtaining any result by reasonable means so as to redress a situation which is intolerable for the German people and the German nation.

Both excerpts cited in Lindley Fraser, *Germany between two wars: A study of propaganda and war guilt* (London, Humphrey Milford, 1944), p 128

Questions

a Identify 'the grievances' in line 7.

b Explain the historical context of Daladier's reference to Poland's 'readiness' in lines 6–7.

c Explain and briefly comment on Hitler's reference to Poland in lines 11–12.

9   The British Ultimatum

(a) *British Foreign Secretary to German Minister of Foreign Affairs, 3 September 1939, 5 a.m.*

[O]n 1st September I informed you . . . that, unless the German Government were prepared to give His Majesty's Government in the United Kingdom satisfactory assurances that the German Government had suspended all aggressive action against Poland
5   and were prepared promptly to withdraw their forces from Polish Territory, His Majesty's Government in the United Kingdom would . . . fulfil their obligations to Poland.

Although this communication was made more than twenty-four hours ago, no reply has been received but German attacks
10 upon Poland have continued and intensified. I have accordingly the honour to inform you that, unless not later than 11 a.m., British Summer Time, today 3rd September, satisfactory assurances to the above effect have been given by the German Government and have reached His Majesty's Government in London, a state of
15 war will exist between the two countries as from that hour.

(b) *The German reply, 3 September 1939, 11.20 a.m.*

The German Government . . . reject the attempt to force Germany, by means of a demand having the character of an ultimatum, to recall its forces which are lined up for the defence of the Reich, and thereby to accept the old unrest and the old injustice. . . .
20 [W]e shall therefore answer any aggressive action on the part of England with the same weapons and in the same form.

> Both excerpts reproduced in *Documents in the Political History of the European Continent 1815–1939*, ed. G. A. Kertesz (London, Oxford University Press, 1968), pp 504, 507

(c) *A historian's comment*

Future historians will have the unenviable task of dividing the blame for a long series of errors between the successive governments of the country and the ever varying moods of the

25   opposition and public opinion which those governments too often
      weakly followed. It was early in 1939, on Hitler's occupation of
      Prague in violation of the Munich agreement a few months before,
      that the British people and Government woke up to the dread
      realities of the situation into which they had been drifting for
30   twenty years. Even then the pace of rearmament was by no means
      what the crisis required, and the union of parties and full
      development of war effort was only effected after six months of
      actual war. At length England faced supreme danger with her old
      courage, of which she found the symbol in Winston Churchill.
35   So the isolationist movement in America and the pacifist
      movement in Britain between them handed the world over to its
      fate, by permitting the 'unnecessary war' as Winston Churchill
      called it. After the First World War the States of Europe had been
      free and independent; even Poland, Czecho Slovakia, Hungary,
40   the Balkan and Baltic States enjoyed independence, because the
      war that ended in 1918 had resulted in the defeat both of Russia
      and of Germany. Therefore Europe was free, and would be free
      to-day, if there had been no second war. That war . . . resulted in
      the second defeat of Germany but in the triumph of Russia in the
45   East. Many of the States for whose freedom we fought against
      Germany have now lost it to Russia.

          G. M. Trevelyan, *History of England* (London, Longmans,
          third edition, 1952), p 731

Questions

★ *a* What were the British Government's 'obligations to Poland'
        (line 7)?
   b Explain (i) the German Government's reference to 'the old
        unrest and the old injustice' (line 19); (ii) 'the isolationist
        movement in America' (line 35); (iii) 'the pacifist movement in
        Britain' (lines 35–6).
   c '[A] long series of errors' (line 23). What do you think
        Trevelyan intended to suggest by his first sentence in extract *c*?
   d What impression of Trevelyan's attitude to British politics
        during the interwar period do you get from extract *c*? Do you
        find his criticism justified?
   e Comment briefly on the use of the conditional, such as
        Trevelyan's in lines 42–3, in the writing of history.
★ *f* From your knowledge of the interwar period, how far, do you
        think, were Britain and America responsible for the outbreak
        of the Second World War?
★ *g* To what extent and in what ways was the Second World War
        an 'unnecessary war' (line 37)?

10   France Enters the War

(a) Daladier's declaration to the Chamber of Deputies, 2 September 1939

Poland has been the victim of the most brutal aggression. The nations who guaranteed her independence are bound to intervene in her defence. Britain and France are not powers who could renounce or think of renouncing their signature. . . .

5   [W]hat would be the value of the guarantee, which was again renewed at the very moment of aggression against Poland; the guarantee given for our Eastern frontier, our Alsace, our Lorraine, after the denouncing of the guarantees successively given to Austria, Czechoslovakia and Poland? Made more powerful by 10   their conquests, gorged with the spoils of Europe, masters of inexhaustible natural riches, the aggressors would soon turn all their forces against France.

        Reproduced in J. Néré, op cit, pp 352–3

(b) An irrational change in foreign policy?

Why did France adopt two totally different attitudes within the space of one year? Why did she enter the war on account of 15   Poland, while forcing Czechoslovakia to yield? . . .

        Was it military considerations which tipped the balance to one side and then to the other? On one point, indeed, these were more favourable in 1939. At the time of Munich, those responsible for French aviation were entirely pessimistic, but now, according to 20   the Air Minister, France had a modern fighter air force and her bomber aircraft were becoming available. As far as the army was concerned, the General Staff had less reason for confidence, but it did not dare advise against armed intervention. It hoped that the Polish army – helped not only by 'General Winter', but before 25   that, owing to the autumn rains, by 'General Mud' – would be able to hold out until the Spring, which was when British help would become effective.

        From the diplomatic point of view, the situation in 1939 was very different from that of 1938. It is true that the German–Soviet 30   agreement was a hard blow, but after Munich one could hardly count on Russian help in practice. Meanwhile, the British attitude had changed radically. It was hardly possible for France, having spent all her efforts over twenty years to convince Britain of the seriousness of the German danger, to take evasive action at the 35   very moment when Britain decided to face up to it.

        However, the new French attitude should not be explained only by the change in British policy. It must be seen that a new Munich Agreement was literally impossible. The determination of the Poles not to be a party to any compromise left France with one

40 alternative; either to support them or to lose face by failing, not
only morally but officially, to keep her word.

Nevertheless, the debate must be extended: the French
government entered the war not to save Poland – it was not sure
of being able to do so – but because it was from that time on
45 convinced, at least in its majority, that Hitler's ambitions knew no
bounds and that if France abandoned her allies she would soon
have to face direct aggression without any outside help.

J. Néré, op cit, pp 241–2

Questions

a Explain the historical background and significance of the first
  sentence of extract *a*.
b What considerations, do you think, influenced Daladier's
  declaration to the Chamber of Deputies on 'the value of the
  guarantee' (line 5)?
c What reasons are given in extract *b* for France's change of
  attitude 'within the space of one year' (lines 13–14)? Do you
  find these reasons convincing?
d '[A] new Munich Agreement was . . . impossible' (lines 37–8).
  What reasons other than those provided in extract *b* would
  you suggest in support of this statement?
e How does Daladier's declaration in extract *a* bear out Néré's
  remarks in the last paragraph of extract *b*?
★ f Why did the French Government wait until 3 September to
  declare war on Germany?